Oh, What A Lovely War!

A Soldier's Memoir

Stanley Swift

transcribed and edited by

Evelyn A. Luscher

Hellgate Press

Central Point, OR

Oh, What A Lovely War! A Soldier's Memoir

Published by Hellgate Press, an imprint of PSI Research, Inc.
Copyright 1999 by Evelyn A. Luscher

For information or to direct comments, questions, or suggestions regarding this book and other Hellgate Press books, contact:

Editorial Department
Hellgate Press
P.O. Box 3727
Central Point, OR 97502

(541) 479-9464 *telephone*
(541) 476-1479 *fax*
info@psi-research.com *e-mail*

Editor: Janelle Davidson
Book designer: Constance C. Dickinson
Compositor: Jan O. Olsson
Cover designer: Steven Burns
Managing Editor: Constance C. Dickinson

Swift, Stanley, 1914–
    Oh, what a lovely war : a soldier's memoir / Stanley Swift.
       p.   cm.
    Includes index.
    ISBN 1-55571-502-8 (pbk.)
    1. Swift, Stanley, 1914– 2. World War, 1939–1945—Personal narratives, British. 3. Soldiers—Great Britain—Biographgy-. 4. Great Britain. Army—Biography. I. Title.
    D811.S96   1999
    940.54'8141—dc21
    [B]   98-55130

Printed and bound in the United States of America
First edition 10 9 8 7 6 5 4 3 2   Eugene

 Printed on recycled paper when available.

These memoirs are dedicated to:

L. Jelley

L. Carter

H. Clarke

K. S. Ford

Davies

R. J. Jones

T. W. Mead

Singleton

W. A. Robinson

Killed in action, January 1943

Contents

Foreword

by Major General Patrick Cordingley

The Seventh Armoured Division was formed in North Africa at the beginning of the Second World War. It took as its tactical sign the jerboa, or gerbil. This delightful and harmless small creature was known affectionately by the soldiers as the desert rat, hence the Division's nickname, the Desert Rats.

The Division's reputation, that of a fiercely professional and successful formation, was established during the battles in the Western Desert. In 1944, once more under the command of Field Marshal Montgomery, it advanced through Normandy to Belgium and Holland and then in 1945 into Germany, eventually fighting to Berlin. Of this epic march Winston Churchill wrote:

> "Dear Desert Rats! May your glory ever shine! May your laurels never fade! May the memory of your glorious pilgrimage of war never die. It was a march unsurpassed through all the story of war."

With the reduction in size of the British Army in the late '50s, the Seventh Armoured Division was disbanded. It handed over its traditions, its memorabilia, and tactical sign to the Seventh Armoured Brigade. This Brigade has been stationed in northern Germany since 1947. In October 1990, it deployed to Saudi Arabia and fought with the U.S. Seventh Corps in Iraq and Kuwait. In 1994 and 1997, it joined the UN peacekeeping force in Bosnia for six months on each occasion.

The Brigade, once more back at its base in Hohne near Hanover in northern Germany, is equipped with the most modern British equipment, the Challenger 2 tank and the Warrior infantry fighting vehicle.

As a onetime commander of the Brigade, I consider it an honour to be asked to write this foreword. Despite having spent only a brief time at war, during Desert Storm where I witnessed the bond of friendship that grew between the soldiers, it is easy to understand how proud the Second World War veterans must have been of their formations and no more so than the soldiers of the Seventh Armoured Division, the Desert Rats. And here we have the story of one of them.

PATRICK CORDINGLEY

Major General
Commander, Seventh Armoured Brigade, 1988–1991

Foreword

by Brigadier K. A. Timbers

The history of the Royal Regiment of Artillery is really the story of its individual batteries, some formed nearly 300 years ago. They were not grouped into regiments for action until toward the end of the nineteenth century, but since that time, there have been many such regiments within the Royal Artillery, each with its own proud history of action.

Among these is Fifth Regiment Royal Artillery, still part of the Royal Regiment of Artillery today although it has changed both its designation and its equipment over the years. Formed at the outbreak of the Second World War as Fifth Regiment Royal Horse Artillery, it was in the British Expeditionary Force that went to France in March 1940. It had a hard fight back to the beaches at Dunkirk, one of its batteries earning the Honour Title "Hondeghem" for its stand against vastly superior German forces in a little Dutch village of that name.

After re-forming in England, Fifth Regiment went to North Africa in July 1942, joining Eighth Armoured Division in the desert campaign against Rommel's Afrika Corps. There the regiment took its place in the famous Alamein Line, followed in October by the battle of that name that was to mark the turning point in the Desert War. There followed the long, hard slog across North Africa to Tunis, driving Rommel out of Africa. During this period, in late November, Fifth Regiment was regrouped with the Seventh Armoured Division, known far and wide as the Desert Rats because they wore the emblem of the gerbil on their sleeves.

Seventh Armored Division went on to Italy but was pulled out in November 1943 to join the Allied forces preparing to land in northwest Europe for the final assault on Germany. Fifth Regiment landed with the Division on Gold Beach on 7 June 1944. There followed hard fighting to break out of the bridgehead, but eventually the regiment was on its way across northern France to Belgium and the Rhine. With Seventh Armoured Division, it crossed the Rhine and headed north toward Bremen and Hamburg. Fifth Regiment ended the war based in Berlin and taking part in the victory parade there.

Fifth Regiment was clearly a fighting regiment, used to the tough conditions of war, thriving on its successes, and unbowed by the misfortunes of the early years with the BEF [British Expeditionary Force]. These are the conditions that breed strong comradeship, a pride in coping with adversity, and a fierce loyalty to the Royal Regiment. Fifth Regiment has been fortunate in retaining its famous batteries and in keeping its traditions despite all the cuts in the post-war strength of the British Army. The history of Fifth Regiment and its famous batteries is a foundation stone, helping to maintain those traditions.

Keeping that history alive, it helps enormously to have the stories of the men who fought in it. This is such a story, and it will be recorded with pride.

K. A. TIMBERS

Brigadier
Historical Secretary
Royal Artillery Institution

Foreword

by Field-Marshal B. L. Montgomery

The following description and tribute to the Seventh Armoured Division was originally written by Field-Marshal B. L. Montgomery as the foreword to *A Short History: Seventh Armoured Division June 1943–July 1945* by Captain Martin Lindsay and Captain M. E. Johnston, published by Printing and Stationery Service, British Army of the Rhine. It is reprinted here with permission from Viscount Montgomery.

It is with great pleasure that I write this short foreword for the story of the 7th Armoured Division from June 1943 onwards.

The Division began its life in the Western Desert of Egypt; it went through all the varying changes of fortune in the desert campaigns; it fought its way across Africa and up to Italy; it landed in Normandy in June 1944 and fought its way across France, Belgium, Holland, and Germany; it was "in at the kill" in Germany in May 1945.

This is a fine record of which every officer and man in the Division can justly be proud.

Of all the Divisions that have served under my command the 7th Armoured Division has served with me the longest; I have had it under my command from

August 1942 to the present time, except for a break from May 1943 to December 1943. I therefore feel that I know it well.

The Division has always given of its best at all times and has left its dead in many lands between Egypt and Germany. To those who have come through to the end I would quote the words of Pericles when speaking at the funeral of those who died in the defence of Athens:

> "To famous men all the earth is a sepulchre: for their virtues shall be testified not only by the inscription on stone at home but, in all
>
> lands wheresoever, in the written record of the mind, which far beyond any monument will remain with all men everlastingly. Be zealous therefore to emulate them."

B. L. MONTGOMERY

Field-Marshal
Commander-in-Chief, 21 Army Group
Germany, July 1945

Acknowledgments

It has been a great privilege for me to transcribe and edit these memoirs. I wish to give special thanks to Stanley Swift's daughter, Lesley Dalby, and also to Werner and Paul Luscher for their generous assistance in this work.

I wish to thank Viscount Montgomery of Alamein, CBE, for his kind permission to use the foreword written by his father, Field Marshal Montgomery, in the book *A Short History: Seventh Armoured Division June 1943–July 1945.*

Also I wish to acknowledge with thanks The Tank Museum, Bovington, England, for permission to use their archival photographs.

Permission by Major G. R. W. Griffin, Ministry of Defence, Whitehall, London, to use the Desert Rat insignia is also gratefully acknowledged.

EVELYN LUSCHER
sister of Stanley Swift

Biography

Stanley Swift was born in Nottingham, England, and at the age of eighteen moved with his family to Burton Joyce, a village six miles distant.

He was an avid cricketer and played for his home team until the outbreak of World War II in September 1939. He enlisted as a private in the Royal Horse Artillery in the British army in early 1940. He fought in many countries, from the African desert where he was one of Field Marshal Montgomery's famous Desert Rats, through Italy and from the beaches of Normandy, France, through Belgium and Holland to Berlin, Germany.

After the war he returned to Burton Joyce and resided there with his wife and four children, later becoming a successful manager in the Nottingham lace industry.

He spoke little of his war experience but occasionally mentioned some incident or other. These recountings aroused so much interest it was suggested that he record his memoir. Reluctant at first, he eventually agreed to place it on tape. As the tapes grew in number, it became apparent that here was a story, a history so unique— the personal document of a soldier in the field—it was truly war with a human face.

Stanley Swift, Fifth Royal Horse Artillery, Seventh Armoured Division, was awarded the 1939–45 Star, the Africa Star, the Italy Star, the France and Germany Star, the Defence Medal, and the War Medal 1939–45.

He died in April 1996 at the age of eighty-one.

Chapter 1

England

In my twenties in 1938, war seemed to be looming large, but we were all lulled into complacency by Prime Minister Neville Chamberlain's piece of paper which said there would be no war. He had been to see Herr Hitler (I can hear his voice now). I saw him get off the old airplane in London, waving his scrap of paper. Nobody knew what was really on it. We had to believe what he said, and he was right, until September 1939.

My life up until then had been rather devoid of activity and adventure with very little future in my job, and I suppose that the idea of war . . ., well, I had the notion it would be all wonderful, marching to bands and that sort of thing.

In retrospect, I think that perhaps my father might have warned me a little bit about war, after his experience in World War I. But I may not have heeded. I was persuaded by the propaganda. I searched for the band and saw the waving flag, and as I said, the future and the job held little prospect, and so I fell for it all and sent in my application to volunteer to join His Majesty's Services.

I was called for a medical examination. There I was, with dozens of other chaps lined up like naked fledglings, devoid of everything, and within ten seconds we were accepted as A-1. God help us! As long as we could breathe and walk, that was good enough. All I know is that I froze there in that line.

In due time I had notification back that it was His Majesty's pleasure to inform me that I had the choice of the infantry or the artillery. (Imagine, the King dealing with me personally!) Neither of these was what I really wanted, but I thought that if I wait until I am conscripted, I won't have any choice at all. Even then my intuition told me that the artillery sounded less dangerous than the infantry, and so it turned out to be.

So I decided on the artillery, and in March 1940 I had my instructions and railway warrant and a few shillings, some miserly sum, which entitled the powers that then were to say I was a member of His Majesty's forces.

I set off for the Midland Railway Station in Nottingham. Nobody saw me off, no one from my family, and no wife as I was single then. I caught a train to London as I had eventually to go to a place called Borden in Hampshire. I had never heard of the place. It could have been in Timbuktu for all I knew. There were a few chaps on the train who looked as though they were new recruits like myself. We were all deathly silent. It was at last dawning on us, I believe, what we had let ourselves in for.

I arrived at St. Pancras Station in London and went into the Underground as I had to go to Waterloo Railway Station to catch a train to the south coast. At that time the Underground was double Dutch to me. I had been to London several times in the past but had never traveled a great deal on the Underground. Once I got the hang of it, it was fairly simple to follow, and I eventually found the train I needed to take me to Borden. It seemed that everybody had converged at Waterloo. There were whole groups of chaps in the railway carriages, and we were all destined for the same place.

I remember that day quite well. It was almost an April-like day, with showers at Waterloo but fairly warm, so the streets were steaming when the sun came out. When we arrived at Borden we straggled, or rather tumbled, off the train like washing out of a dryer, all creased and crumpled from the showers on our journey. What a motley crew!

There were four or so wagons waiting at the station and a red-faced sergeant who looked as though he had a daily intake of about fifteen pints of beer. He tried to line us up into some sort of order. Then he said something like "left turn," and everybody turned this way and that. You found yourself facing your neighbor or banging into somebody else. Never mind, we were just beginners. Then we clambered up—we were hardly agile—the backboard of what we found out was called a five-tonner. We were counted off in groups as we all piled in—the first time we were being regimented. At least there were enough vehicles for us, which seemed rather good organization, and far better than the army in general, as we found out later. Off we trundled, passing soldiers walking about looking most military. I think it was a Saturday.

Arriving at the camp, we drove through the entrance gate, past the guardroom, and down to the front of a relatively new brick building three stories high. The ground floor was for the newest intake, we discovered, the second was for soldiers who'd trained for a month, and the third was for the two-month trainees. You moved up, ladderlike, and of course the chaps who'd been there one month and moved to the second floor looked at us nonchalantly. They were real soldiers, old-timers, and the people on the third floor were the real McCoy, trained, raring-to-go soldiers.

We straggled in. The first thing we had to cope with was that we were late for what they called dinner. We went into the mess hall, and tables were laid out, ten to a table, four on each side, one on each end. The poor devil who got the end seat was the table orderly automatically, and he went with great pangs of misgiving to the long kitchen counter. There sat a large pan filled with stew, congealing greasily. He had an almost guilty look on his face as he carried it back to us.

It was a memorable meal. Our appointed orderly plonked the pan on the table and ladled stew onto our plates, which were metal. The mass was stone cold and looked like something the dog had thrown up. None of us touched any of it. It all went back. Well, at least we didn't have to wash up. Two weeks later, presented with the same food, we gobbled it up and looked for more. That's how things changed.

The ATS (Auxiliary Territorial Service) girl who retrieved the pan was, I think, the ugliest girl in England. Perhaps she was particularly tired after a day of cooking, but her face ... well, everything was wrong with it. Fortunately for her, she was in the minority. Girls were few and far between here, and as we found out later, chaps were chasing after her right, left, and center. But she was interested only in sergeants and above. It seemed to me that proportion was all wrong, one woman to ten or so men. That creates a terrible imbalance. She was able to pick and choose, so she looked at us with total disdain, as mere civilians trying to become soldiers.

When we first arrived at the barracks, the sergeant presented a formidable list with everybody's name typed on it. There was absolutely no way of escaping. We all began to hope, I'm sure, that somehow our name wouldn't be on the list and we could go back home again. But there your name was Mr. So-and-So.

At the same time we were given a rank—Mr. So-and-So no longer—and a number. We were now soldiers. Officially I was now Gunner S. Swift, 973307 (a number that is etched into my very soul), Twelfth Field Training Regiment, Royal Artillery, Borden, Hampshire. It looked most impressive on paper.

Then we were marched off to our dormitory. It looked fairly homely. The wooden floor was highly polished. (We found out later who had to do the polishing.) Lockers were beside each bed. We each staked our claim, and then it was off to the quartermaster's store. There everything under the sun was thrown at us. First we were given a huge kit bag, then shorts (two), undershirts (two), shirts (three), webbing, straps, brass button holders, and a "housewif," which turned out to be a housewives sewing kit.

Everything was screamed at us. It was like a comic opera, most musical: trousers, khaki; drill belt, khaki; jacket, khaki; cap, khaki; two of those; one for best; and khaki-drill for when we did maintenance work—scraggy, shapeless articles of clothing. And then a metal helmet was plonked on our heads.

It turned out later that the jacket collar in every case would have fitted a Charolais bull. It was about a seventy-two-inch neck, and the front of it hung to your navel. I suppose they were manufactured all one size to cater to everybody, from the most stringy neck to the most beefy. Later we had to go to a tailor who in some miraculous way adjusted them to fit, but for the rest we still looked a mess. Trousers were either so long that you dragged the bottoms or so short that they finished halfway up your calves. You never saw such a raggle-taggle mob in all your life.

There we were with our separate piles. We didn't know where anything was supposed to go. Finally we were given three blankets for our bed. The common look on everybody's face was perplexity, astonishment, uncertainty. Then we went with all this unfathomable conglomeration back to our barracks.

A nice, kind sergeant came and showed us how to fold the blankets neatly, one on top of the other. We had to sew a little strip of oil canvas on each blanket to write our name and rank on, so that when the blanket was folded the strip would show. We later learned that heaven help you if your blankets weren't in line, one on top of the other. All hell was let loose.

Then we were sent to the doctor who injected us against every tropical disease known to man. The sergeant, who was still kindly, said, "You'd better bed down now over the weekend," and we thought, how nice, how considerate. We couldn't see any particular reason for this solicitousness. A half hour later we knew. Everybody was knocked out flat. We thought this must be the worst the army has to offer, that it can't be any worse than this, being half-killed by lethal injection.

Came Monday we were recovered, and this kindly sergeant turned into a raging tornado, a foul, evil monster, mouthing the worst obscenities imaginable. He tumbled us out, dressed in this queer garb we'd acquired, and we had our first taste of army life. We were going to have a course of drill, and there was a program drawn up: drill, PT (physical training), drill, drill, drill, arms drill, more drill, and so it went.

The parade ground was a vast square in front of the buildings, and there were several squads already marching on it. There we formed up in rows of three, about ten to a row.

I must mention here that at the end of each month, the sergeants created a competition, and the best-drilled squad earned the sergeant a medal or some commendation. Our sergeant had been winning all the time. By God, he was determined that we wouldn't break his record!

The damned great army boots were a bane. The leather was dimpled, hard as iron, and we had to "bone them down" with the handle of a toothbrush and keep spitting on the toecap, rub in boot polish, then continue rubbing with the toothbrush handle, over and over. We'd spit and polish, spit and polish. With the passage of time, we smoothed the boots and made them shine. We were given blanco, a greenish type of chalk which when dipped in water became a liquid mass. We had to blanco our equipment and polish our brass, which was a gorgeous shade of green when we received it, and clean and spit and polish some more. It was punishment of the first order. And it was evil the way we were expected to do everything in ten minutes and turn out on parade. But it had a purpose; it made us subservient, mindless cogs, obedient robots, good soldiers.

The boots weighed a ton, and we thumped our feet hard enough on the concrete of the parade ground to sink holes every time we turned. We marched forward and backward, right turned, left turned, right wheeled, left wheeled, and oh, our feet did ache.

Of course there were always idiots in the group. (If I'd only realized what it took to get out of the army I would have become one, too.) These people couldn't start by swinging the left arm forward with the right foot forward; it didn't come automatically. They couldn't get it right. And they couldn't respond to drill orders about turning. They'd go marching off in the wrong direction instead of turning like everyone else. They were weeded out and sent back to some easy job somewhere in the north of Scotland, presumably, out of the way. (My God, if I'd only learned to march badly!)

After we'd finished our marching up and down, we were bawled at to return to barracks to prepare for PT. There we whipped off our clothes and put on our PT kit, white vest, blue short drawers which finished down below our knees, and plimsolls. How ludicrous we looked. (Had Hitler seen us, he would have laughed all the way to Berchtesgaden.) Then off we dashed to the gym, barging up and down, running about, knee bends, stretch, press up, press down. Oh, what a life, what physical dexterity. Then dash back to barracks, with five minutes to get dressed and out again.

At ten o'clock we were given a break for a smoke, as if it was a great gift from heaven. The NAAFI (Navy, Army, and Air Force Institution) van came along with the inevitable cry, "Tea and a wad." Tea and a bun. Tea so thick you could stand your spoon in it.

And so it went on for a month, all this nonsense, as well as learning how to salute and say "Sir" every two seconds to our superiors. We weren't allowed outside the area of the barracks until we'd completed this month's training, until we'd been made real soldiers—at least until we looked it.

As part of our training we had to do a course of night guard in front of the guardroom. We stood at ease with our rifle, as per drill, at the most unusual angle when it came to "slope arms." These instructions confused me completely. Standing there perfectly still, the rifle at the correct angle to my body like a toy soldier, my wrists would ache like hell. As I stood this guard I soon found out that, if I stood still for more than five minutes, a stentorian voice from inside the guardroom would bawl, "Move up and down! Move up and down!" So I had to come to attention, slope arms, march up and down ten paces that way, about turn, ten paces this way, and so on for hours.

Almost a month into our basic training, we suddenly had our first experience of war. Everything had been straightforward, chaps barging up and down on the parade ground, smarter every day. Then to spoil it all, early one gorgeous morning out of the sun, dive-bombers came shooting down. They seemed to be aiming for our brick barracks. I was on the toilet, fortunately on the ground floor, and the first bomb came whizzing down, just missed the building, and demolished a row of wooden huts which had been used as sleeping quarters. I shot out of the lavatory, trousers around my ankles, looking wildly for a place of safety. I was hobbled by fear, never mind trousers, and palsied by my first taste of war.

After that it became a practice of the Luftwaffe to disturb us through the night by sending over bombers in single file to drop bombs at random. This sometimes went on for most of the night hours. (The only consolation was that the Germans were losing their sleep, too.) We had to proceed to the air-raid shelters, and the formal drill was that we were required to put our gas masks on. At all clear, when we came out of the shelter we had to line up for roll call. The sergeant major started shouting our names while he still had his gas mask on. You never heard such a muffled mumble in all your life.

Our first month came to an end, and we were real soldiers. We were smart, things fitted, the collar was reasonable, and we were allowed out. Visualize how calves and lambs released from their winter quarters throw their rear legs in the air and jump and prance about. That was us.

We would go out in twos and threes, and if we saw an officer approaching, we counted silently: one, two, three, salute. Like automatons our arms would shoot up in martial unison. Then we conceived the idea of spacing ourselves far enough apart to keep this chappie busy. The officer, poor devil, would be saluting every five seconds. How else could we exert a little revenge?

As well as winning limited freedom, we moved upstairs and were veterans. We saw the new intake of civilians arrive. They were identical copies of us a month ago, all going into the great machine to be molded, pressed, formed, modeled, and churned out in exactly the same style, shape, and personality.

And so it went on. We were given lectures about how we must uphold the magnificent record the regiment had had through the centuries, how wonderful it was to die for King and Country, and how to avoid naughty women.

One of the great moments of army life was the ritual of pay parade. It was conducted in alphabetical order, done that way, no doubt, since the Battle of Bannockburn. The officer, in all his pomposity, sat at a green, baize-covered table with the money. I was well down the list, but when the sergeant called my name, I marched up, saluted, held out right hand for one pound, eight shillings, about-turned, and marched briskly away. That was the formula—all so frightfully formal.

I am left-handed, and once in a moment of forgetfulness, I held out that hand for my pay. The sergeant yelled "Swift! Swift! Right 'and out!" I looked at him with the most childlike expression I could muster, begging forgiveness. You couldn't upset the formula.

One early payday a chap named Phillips was waiting in his rightful alphabetical place. When he got to the Fs, the sergeant screamed, "Phillips! Phillips! The Fs! It's the Fs! Get in place!" Oh God! Brains!

We also endured the ritual of kit inspection every Saturday lunchtime. Everything had to be clean and shipshape, floor a mirror, lockers dust free, nothing left out. Three blankets with tapes showing on the front, all in line, mess tins on top, spare pair of boots face up, dazzling. Kit bag turned out, contents laid in precise marching order: cotton vest, PT shorts, spare shirts neatly rolled up. Missing articles of clothing were "in the laundry, Sir." Everybody lost something. We had a very busy laundry.

Once a chap lost his shaving brush and said to his friends, "I've lost my shaving brush," and then mysteriously one turned up. Shortly afterwards another fellow complained his shaving brush was missing, and so it went down the line until the last poor sap was minus a shaving brush with nobody to turn to. Petty thievery was rife, especially near inspection time.

During our third month, we were introduced to the guns. They were Boer War vintage, possibly, or First World War. We couldn't touch them; we just had to look at them. They'd been shined and polished. They looked wonderful. We were told which was the entrance for the shell to go into and which was the exit for the shell to emerge and how the gun swivelled. We could hardly wait to get our own toy.

My time at Borden coincided with the retreat from Dunkirk. We received hundreds of men. They were ragtag, dirty, unshaven, but with a certain nobility, as if they felt down but not really out. They'd gone without sleep, their eyes were dull, and they were all mixed together, nobody belonging to any unit. Everything was a complete shambles.

These men were provided with what we called biscuits, three mattress squares, which when laid out made a full-length bed. We piled these inside the gun park, which was a huge shed where the guns were kept. That was their accommodation until the dust settled and these men were sorted out into their old regiments and moved on.

It was then decided to dig a massive tank trap across southern England, presumably in the event of invasion. We were given a section to complete. We bulldozed trees and dug and dug. It was a most beautiful summer that year, and I was as fit as I have ever been in my life.

We were in southern command, and General Montgomery was in charge. He was a fitness fanatic and ordained that every man, officers and other ranks alike, do a five-mile run every week. As ordered, we all set off running. Then some canny individuals after a short distance dropped out by the wayside, had a leisurely smoke, and waited for the zealots coming back, then joined the pack, putting on a wonderful act of panting and staggering. But that ruse didn't last long. We were taken out in trucks, dropped off five miles away, and ordered to run back. We even beat that system. If we were lucky, we would catch a lift from a vehicle going in our direction, but that was difficult to do, so we were left with little choice.

At the end of our training we were allowed our first leave. I traveled to Nottingham with a friend who also hailed from there. We thought, being real soldiers, we'd go to a pub before going home, and we did. We had too much to drink, and I was incapable of getting to my final destination, Burton Joyce, a village several miles away.

Fortunately, in the pub I saw a lady who worked at my old firm—as well as you could see anybody in the haze of cigarette smoke—with a female friend. The befuddled reality of my plight set in, and I asked her if she'd be kind enough to let me sleep on her couch. She said she would. I went with her with not much memory of the journey. Her husband was at home, a big, white-haired, retiring sort of man, and a daughter, and it all seemed very hospitable, considering. My hostess showed me the front room, which boasted a couch which seemed to me quite adequate for sleeping, and later, to my surprise, joined me there.

It began to dawn on me that her motives were not quite beyond reproach. I was nonplussed by the activities and began to realize that I was in a rather perilous situation. So I made a rather hasty exit, somewhat sobered, and at the crack of dawn the warrior went home to Burton Joyce.

I had a week's leave and dreamt of *Paradise Lost*. One evening I again went into a pub in Nottingham, so packed that nobody bothered about chaps in uniform. I queued up and finally got to the bar. There was beer but no glasses to drink it from. I finally got a glass, then the beer ran out. And that's how the leave went.

On my return to His Majesty's forces, I found myself at Waterloo Station in the middle of one of the earliest and heaviest air raids. No trains were running, so I was presented with the problem of having to stay the night in London and find a way to get back to Borden the following morning. It was a night I'll never forget.

I wandered around and went down into the underground tube station. It was absolutely packed with humanity: men, women, and children. Everybody was trying to be brave and courageous and singing, *"We'll Hang Out the Washing on the Siegfried Line."* Poor souls, some of them looked as though they needed a wash themselves. There was no future there, so I drifted back up to the street again. I found I was standing near an overhead steel railway bridge, and underneath was a tea, coffee, and sandwiches stall. The chap there was still serving in the middle of the air raid. I stood listening to the falling bombs and the clatter of anti-aircraft shrapnel falling back to earth. It was altogether a most unpleasant night. The German Luftwaffe seemed to be making a concerted effort to decimate that part of London.

The next morning I was able to get a bus to Clapham Junction and from there get to Borden, arriving a day late. All the chaps, all my friends, had already gone. They'd left the day before. So there I was, this solitary soul without a friend in the world. I asked if I could join them, but the army bureaucracy said no. I would have to wait a further month and twiddle my thumbs until it was time for the next gang to go. So I lost my unit completely. (Years later I met a Nottingham man who'd been in my original group who told me that they'd been sent to the far east, to India, Siam, and Burma, where they'd had a very rough time. So who knows why fate changed my course.)

My new group was posted to a holding regiment, which meant that we were fully trained and were standing by, ready to fill any vacancies or any new regiments that were being formed. We were sent to Ascot racecourse, and there we had to sleep in the stands and run around the racecourse every morning. Fortunately, we didn't have to carry a jockey on our backs.

The blitzkrieg on London continued. Enemy planes flew over our encampment quite low, and at night we saw the flames and knew how badly the city was getting it. Chaps who had families there were really concerned. The east end, the docks, bore the brunt one night. Everything was ablaze, oil, food storage warehouses; it was a most awe-inspiring and terrible sight, an amazingly effective raid. After their attack, the returning planes flew over us, in the comparative safety of Ascot, where we felt so helpless.

With the approach of winter our unit was posted to Burton-on-Trent, a great beer-brewing center, and we were housed in a vacant brewing warehouse, a large, empty room with beds laid out on the floor. I'd already had a leave, but suddenly a notice appeared on the board that I was due for further leave. The difficulty was that it had been noted in my army book that I'd already had leave. But being a regular, seasoned soldier, full of cunning and craft, I eradicated the writing with breadcrumbs. It was so obvious, really, to anyone looking carefully. But my book was duly stamped, I was issued with a railway warrant, and I went back home again.

When I returned, a fatal list was posted with my name on it. We were to join some regiment totally unknown to us which had been decimated in the fall of France and the withdrawal from Dunkirk. And so my fate was ordained. This was to be my regiment for the rest of the war, the Fifth Royal Horse Artillery. We had no horses, of course; by this time everything was mechanized. We thought we were a cut above the ordinary Royal Artillery, but I don't think we were, really.

We arrived about 3:00 A.M. at Coggeshall, somewhere in the middle of nowhere in the south of England, and we were immediately told to blanco our webbing as it was the wrong color for the regiment. At 3:00 A.M!

We shuttled about, first moving to a place called Great Dunmow, where we were housed in a supposedly haunted vicarage, although we never saw any ghosts. Sometimes after we'd been to the pub, I doubt we'd have recognized a ghost had we seen one. Perhaps they preferred more genteel company than us, clomping about. It was quite cold by then, wintry, and I recall our metaled boots ringing on the ground as we walked to the nearest pub in the evening. The place was packed with RAF (Royal Air Force) personnel as there was an aerodrome nearby, but we melded in somehow. Our stay in Great Dunmow was brief, however. We were ordered up north to a place called Silsden in Yorkshire.

Off we went, our convoy taking two days to get there. Fortunately, it was a wonderful move. Silsden was a very small village, and we were the first soldiers to be billeted there, in a woolen mill. The villagers welcomed us with open arms, especially the girls.

I became good friends with one particular fellow named Larry Jelley, and we often went into the nearest town, Keighley, and whooped it up, all on about a shilling each. Most times that was all we had between us. We frequented the milk bar opposite the bus station, put a penny in the jukebox, listened to the sentimental songs, and pined for a world that would never be. We'd have a milk shake each and make it last as long as we possibly could.

One evening we were there, Larry and I and another bloke called Nobby Clarke, when a couple of girls came in, which was rather unfortunate because two girls and three men hardly works out. They were most pleasant girls, sisters, Marion and Hillary. We chatted casually, and it appeared they had good jobs in one of the mills there. They must have realized that we were financially strapped, and always were, for they slipped us a ten shilling note, which was a fortune then. So we decided to live it up and grace the Station Hotel, a posh place, with our presence. There we sat in the lounge, among the red tabs, colonels and majors and Lord knows what, with waiters dressed like penguins delivering our drinks. Ten bob did buy a couple of rounds for five people. We were indeed living!

They were wonderful girls, and we met them many times when we were there. They couldn't do enough for us, and on Christmas Day 1940 they invited us to tea. The three of us went, Larry, Nobby, and myself, and the table was as festive as anyone could wish. Their father, a stalwart man, was interested in brass bands and very knowledgeable about them as were many in that part of the country. All brass band people. During the meal they introduced us to a mixture of cheese and cake, a strongly flavored Christmas cake and a strongly flavored cheese. The admixture seemed strange, but it really worked; it was delicious.

I went on leave from Silsden. It was the only time I wasn't sorry to get back to camp after my leave was over. That shows how pleasant the place was.

Then came the fateful day when we had to leave Silsden. We traveled in convoy down south to Wiltshire, a heck of a long way. We traveled quite slowly and en route passed near Burton Joyce. It almost broke my heart to be so close to home and yet so far. We went through Leicester and stayed overnight in an open-air camp at Lutterworth, where we were regaled with the inevitable and constant stew, the menu of choice.

In due course we arrived in Wiltshire and were housed in Nissen huts on some nob's estate, but our stay was brief. The only memories of note of that stay were going into the town of Hungerford with Larry, having a meal of egg and chips, and standing on the bridge of a river there, watching dozens and dozens of trout so tame one had the feeling the fish would just beg to give themselves up if you threw in a fishing line.

Again we moved, to Dorking, a place where we would stay and train for a year. We were billeted in a great mansion owned by landed gentry, who also owned huge tracts of slum property in London. They'd been heroic: they'd departed for America and left the place to the army.

We were now part of a division. We were all dressed up with divisional signs on our arms, and we trained as a divisional group. For a short time we had no guns at all, but one day they did arrive, to great rejoicing. I don't know why we were so pleased about that, but we were. We thought these weapons were wonderful. Wonderful! We were brainwashed already.

Our officers were housed in the palatial quarters in which the owners once lived and we were billeted in the servant's quarters, attics to which we climbed back stairs. Social distinction was rigorously observed in our mansion. But it was a pleasant enough stay.

We had to do guard duty, and there's nothing more soul destroying than having to do a twenty-four-hour guard, with all the ritualistic hooha. We were given the afternoon free from other duties in order to clean ourselves up, polish our brass, make sure our rifle was clean, put on our best uniform. At the pre-scribed time we'd line up, a bombardier or sergeant in charge, and go through the drill ritual, slope arms, present arms, all that nonsense. The bore of our rifle was examined to ensure its cleanliness, then off we marched to the guard we were about to relieve where we were inspected by the orderly officer. We were not allowed to speak to the officer unless spoken to. If we wanted to speak to a higher-ranking man, a major for instance, first of all we had to see the sergeant, he saw the lieutenant, the lieutenant saw the captain, and so it went.

I recall vividly a bank of bluebells outside the guardhouse. In the early hours as the first tendrils of sunlight appeared and grew, the bank became one luminous, shimmering sheet of blue. It was beautiful. Guard duty did have its compensations.

Sometimes it even had its funny side. The guard detail was supposed to be always dressed and ready for instant emergency, and of course we weren't. When it wasn't our turn to be tramping up and down outside, we would release our restric-tive webbing equipment and try to take a nap. We were in our normal state of dis-array when for some strange reason the colonel decided to do an early inspection. He was an aristocrat, the commanding officer, resplendent in a beautifully cut uniform. He sniffed constantly as though he'd got something under his nose and not very pleasant at that. We all tumbled out. Everybody was barking and shouting, and the orderly officer was looking most embarrassed at our disheveled state. The bombardier in charge of us came straggling out, straightened up, presented arms to the colonel, and said smartly, "Sorry, sir, but what can you expect on one sausage for supper and breakfast?"

The colonel turned to the orderly officer and said severely, "*One* sausage for breakfast for these chaps? Make sure they get another one." And we did.

The man in charge of the guard had a book in which he was supposed to record anything unusual that happened. There was nothing in it because nothing ever happened. But one day an entry did appear: *3:00 A.M. Accidentally kicked over tea bucket. Straightened tea bucket. Saluted tea bucket.*

When on guard duty, it was your job to wake the cook. A word about this particular cook. He was a gray-faced, truculent man. I don't know where he came from, perhaps nowhere as he was a regular soldier, perhaps born in the army. He was the dirtiest man I ever saw. He wore dirty denims and a vest that had so many holes it looked like lace. The color was anything but white. Nobody bothered him; he was beyond any official censure. He had to arise extremely early and often prepare sandwiches for the lot of us if we went out on an exercise. He had the inevitable stew waiting for us when we returned, and so we had no regular mealtimes but ate whenever the opportunity arose. To wake the cook was not the most pleasant task at five o'clock in the morning.

First order of the day was to make tea. Hot, strong, and sweet, it was made in a bucket. This handy utensil was stainless steel, holding about three gallons, and the procedure was to throw in the tea, pour on boiling water, and then add Libby's condensed milk. For speed a hole was punched in a couple of Libby's cans and then cans and all tossed into the brew. In time the labels would detach, float to the surface, and be scooped out. When the tea was finished, empty cans were fished from the bottom of the bucket. Most efficient.

We had to engage in sports events, presumably so called to enhance our fighting spirit. I was designated to box a certain sergeant ominously nicknamed Mr. Punch. You never saw such an oddly matched pair, eight stone wet through— that was me—against twelve stone of muscle and sinew. The captain was our referee, a handsome bloke with a youthful, soft, pink complexion. He tried to look firm and solemn and captainlike, and to do that he grew a moustache, which made him look like a character from *The Chocolate Soldier*.

So there I was, being prepared for my title fight, having boxing gloves tied on my hands. I'd never worn boxing gloves before, and I could hardly lift my puny arms because of their weight. My opponent was prancing around, a wildcat, a fiend, looking most professional. He danced toward me, and I started grinning at him. The more I grinned, the more he hopped, and the referee shouted, "Stop! Stop! Gunner Swift wipe that grin off your face!"

I said, "But sir, it's the only defense I have. It's riling him, and he's missing me!"

We started again, and he never could land a blow on me. We were both getting more and more angry, he from frustration and I from the injustice of it all, but I kept grinning and ducking and weaving and backing. I wasn't going to get anywhere near him. All I wanted was to keep out of trouble.

There was no end to it. I had to box a chap called Bennett, a poor, retiring lily of a fellow who should never have been in the army. He was delicate and had a slight stutter, and I was so steamed up I thought, "I'll take it out of you, you sod!" I pasted him right and left, and he cried, "Swifty! S-Swifty! Stop! What're you d-doing that for?" I dropped another punch and said, "You'll find out." Cruel, but victory was sweet.

At the side of our mansion was a large garage containing two Rolls Royce motorcars in pristine condition. They were beautiful machines, both jacked up off the floor to protect the tires, obviously carefully preserved for future use by the owners. Next to the garage was our cookhouse. Now, we were all aware that one of our orderlies appeared to have an IQ of minus four, and his vocabulary was composed of ooh, ah, and um. This articulate fellow wanted to light a fire, so he found an oily rag in the garage and lit it. The garage floor happened to be old and wooden, the planks having shrunk leaving gaps between, and this chap accidentally dropped the flaming rag between the gaps and set the garage on fire.

We all rushed to the scene of disaster led by our sergeant major, a highly strung man with a frantic attitude. He screamed for a pickax, which somebody dutifully brought him. He swung one mighty swing to knock the jacks from under the first car, missed the jack, and smashed the pickax straight into the radiator of the Rolls Royce. Fortunately, we did manage to push both cars out, but one Rolls Royce wasn't quite as pristine. The owners would be pleased.

This incident did nothing for the sergeant's nerves, a peculiar bloke who looked more like Punch, of *Punch and Judy*, than Punch himself. He possessed glaring eyes, a hooked nose, slit mouth, and his jaw and chin were a crescent moon. Had he been a puppet, his face would have kept children giggling for hours. But he was an unfortunate man. (Later when we were in Africa fighting in the western desert his nerves collapsed completely, and he bit off all the fingers of one hand. We never saw him again.)

Now that we had our guns, brand-new, straight from the factory, we started training in earnest. My job as gun layer was to realign the gun after each firing. When it was fired, the gun reared up and lost its line completely, and so with instruments I lined the gun up again on its main objective and when necessary readjusted its range.

We dashed around the village of Stamford. It was a ghost village as all the residents had been turned out and relocated. We smashed the place up with cannon and tank fire, bashing into things and making a mess of everything. The people were supposed to go back there after the war, but unfortunately, we left nothing to go back to.

We went all over on maneuvers. Lark Hill, a firing range on Salisbury Plain, had miles and miles of open space so that we could show off our guns and what they could do. The generals enjoyed the display more than anyone. In the winter of 1941–1942, we had finished firing in the early hours of the morning and received no further instructions. Tired, I sat with my back to the wheel of the gun in about a foot of snow. The desolation there at that time had to be seen to be believed. And so we waited, frozen to the bone, forgotten, it seemed, by the generals and everybody.

The weather gradually improved, and we were on an exercise near Stonehenge. The sun had just risen, and I looked down into the valley and saw the noble spire of Winchester Cathedral seeming to reach into the very heavens. I was overcome with awe that men, hundreds of years ago with limited equipment, could build something of such magnificence. I wondered what we would leave for future generations.

But there was little time for lofty thoughts. Guns were our life, and we were getting to know how to use them. When the gun fired, it reared up and came down with a crash, and if you were not careful, it would land on your knee, and that was extremely painful. You learned to keep yourself out of the way.

Once we were lifting the gun up. It was a counter-balanced type of situation. Once you'd got the trail at the end up, it was in perfect balance. One person could perhaps hold it quite easily with one finger. But if you lost that balancing force, you were in trouble. So two of us, one on each side, held the gun tilted up, ready to swivel it around. The bloke on the other side—I was muggins (the simpleton) holding it on my side—either let go or ceased to use any power of persuasion, with the consequence that I couldn't hold the gun and it dropped on my big toe.

The damage to me was such that I was admitted to the Cottage Hospital at Dorking. There I was tended by a young nurse, a beautiful girl in my eyes, and had my toenail removed. The nail never grew again, and I've since regarded that big toe with great affection because it got me a week off duty.

Some weeks later someone organized a dance for us, and I invited my beautiful nurse and asked her to bring a friend for Larry. The evening passed pleasantly enough, considering neither Larry nor I could dance; we weren't the most debonair of chaps. When it was time to leave, we looked forward to a pleasurable, leisurely good-bye. It was inevitable, I suppose, but sometime during the evening the girls had become acquainted with a sergeant and his friend, who outranked us and probably could dance, as well. So our companions took off with superior rank, leaving two rather miffed lowly gunners behind. So much for fidelity. (Later this same sergeant was killed at a rather awful time in the western desert in Africa. I saw him at a distance. He was sitting in his jeep when a huge shell landed and shrapnel went through the back seat of the jeep, and that was the end of him.)

Our military exercises continued, once taking us near Brighton. We had a beautiful view of the English channel but not much time to admire the view or the wonders of nature. We were parked on a hill, having a bit of trouble with our vehicle and the attached gun. German planes suddenly appeared, probably on their way to bomb London. We heard whistling sounds and immediately dove for cover. Well, to say the Germans have no sense of humour is tommyrot. Empty bottles fell out of the sky whistling just like bombs and crashed all around us. They put the fear of God into us as these missiles clattered and smashed. Splintered glass was flying all over the place. Had they been actual bombs they would have made direct hits. Guardian Angel number one.

One evening we were given leave to go into town. The beach was closed, barbed wired. Nobody was allowed there any more. A cinema in town was still functioning, showing Walt Disney's *Fantasia*. I was absolutely enthralled, completely transported. I had never seen anything like it, the admixture of music and colorful riotous imagination. What an escape from the regimented world!

The powers that were in London hadn't given much thought to our sanitary requirements while we were engaged in exercises. The method of dealing with bodily functions was quite medieval. Sanitary orderlies dug a huge pit about ten yards long and five feet deep. On either end of this hole were two wooden beams which supported a long plank on which you sat, with a pole at your back to lean against. You had a constant dread of slipping off the plank into the malodorous mess beneath. First thing in the morning before breakfast this was a particularly gregarious spot.

Back at camp, a frequent duty was to clean all the vehicles. After cleaning we wiped them down with some sort of engine oil until they shone as though they'd just come from the showroom. But three of us, Larry, Nobby, and myself, found a way of avoiding all this work. As long as you looked busy, nobody took particular notice of you. So we picked up our buckets, filled them with dirty, oily cloths, put on bright, expectant, workaday expressions, and dashed here and there until we reached the end of the track. Then we'd disappear into the adjoining woods where nearby was a small cafe. We'd spend half an hour there having a cup of tea and reappear just as the vehicle inspection was over. We did that week after week, and nobody ever missed us.

Another duty assigned to us was to bring cows in from the field each evening, and in due course it fell to my lot, a townee, to get those damn cows into their shed. I hadn't the foggiest notion how to go about it. Should I call, "Maisie," or whistle or thump them on the rear or what? They were all over the field, and I sort of maneuvered myself behind them, trying to corral them. They'd be out to this day, but a countryman used to handling such beasts came along and had them in in no time. Why the army gave us such tasks is beyond me.

Larry and I were inseparable, always together, as our tastes were very similar, although he spoke very little about his past life. All I knew was that he came from Wales and before the war had worked in the kitchen of a London hotel. I never learned anything about his parents and understood vaguely that he'd had an association with a girl in London and had had some problems, probably the cause of his reticence. But we both enjoyed the countryside and, time and duty permitting, would go out at dusk and hear the nightingales sing. It seemed so peaceful, far removed from the rigors of camp, remote from war. We did a lot of walking in the Surrey countryside and one day were crossing a newly cut cornfield when suddenly from the stubble a grouse shot up with a great whirring of wings, startling us more than we'd startled him.

We sometimes ended up at a pub in a nearby village whenever we had a shilling between us for half a pint. Larry and I were quiet, well-behaved, and all we wanted was a bit of conversation with the locals. But disappointingly, it seemed they didn't want to know us. Usually, we were ignored, and we had the feeling that we were regarded as somewhat inferior, or perhaps it was that they somehow resented having to put up with so many troops impacting their lives. Whatever the reason, the welcome and warmth we'd received from people in the north of England were absent here.

At the end of a year, we were thoroughly trained, ready, and raring to go. We were told that we were going abroad and given embarkation leave. To say a shiver ran through the ranks was an understatement. We all went on leave. An Irishman in our regiment had to go home in civilian clothes as he was from southern Ireland. Of course, he never came back. He knew what was in store.

My leave was memorable. I was married to a girl I had loved a long time. She had enlisted in the WAAF (Women's Auxiliary Air Force), and ours was a church wedding in uniform. My sister, also in the WAAF, was bridesmaid, and my fiancée's brother, in the RAF, was best man. We spent a brief honeymoon in Matlock, Derbyshire, before we returned to our respective stations.

Back at Dorking preparations for our departure were complete. We had a final medical examination. Of our trio, Nobby Clarke was found to have bad feet, at that late stage, and pronounced unfit to go. He was posted elsewhere, and I never saw him again.

Came the great day we were due to go. Then about a mile away an ammunition dump blew up, and everybody in the vicinity was supposed to help put out the fires. However, as we were being shipped abroad, we couldn't participate; but it made for an exuberant send-off.

There was a long driveway from our mansion to the road. We lined up there with all our kit and were supposed to get into an imaginary train standing beside the driveway, six men to each carriage. There we were, sorting ourselves into sixes and walking into mythical railway carriages. The idiocy of it!

We eventually departed from some obscure place on the railway line, nowhere near a station. We certainly went in secret. We had no idea where we were going as we sat all jammed in with equipment and everything and the few rations we'd been given. The train set off in the afternoon, and in the evening, believe it or not, we stopped at Nottingham Midland Station. My home! But there were military police at all the exits. Nobody was likely to leave. We stayed there until the early hours of the morning.

We finally arrived on the Clyde in Scotland. The journey had taken thirty hours, and we arrived the following night. In the middle of that night we embarked on the troopship. It was nothing like a Hollywood leave-taking with flags waving, streamers, bands playing, and relatives on the quayside waving a tearful farewell. The place was dark and deserted, with only three hooded lights on the quayside because of air-raid danger. Three or four dockers in black, dingy clothes stood there. The tide was in, the ship was riding high, and the gangplank was at a precarious angle. One bloke dropped his kit as he was negotiating the steep climb, and the sergeant yelled obscenities at him that he was holding everybody up. A vast mass of sympathy seemed to go out to the unfortunate chap, and I had the feeling then that there was a man who wouldn't survive the war.

When we were all on board, we were issued with a one-page form letter on which to write our loves ones that we were leaving. And that was all. A soldier came along gathering up the forms we'd written and moved off with the bundle.

I suddenly felt envious due to the fact that to him it meant nothing; he was going back on land.

Then the hawsers were cast off. The stevedores on shore turned away without the slightest farewell gesture. They'd probably seen it all before. In that instant I felt as though we were lepers and the entire country was ashamed of us. We were sneaking away furtively, everybody glad to see us gone. It was a most depressing emotion, but everything contrived to foster it. Silently we moved on the filthy, oily water and floating debris. Everybody seemed depressed and sad. It was nothing like I'd expected.

I had thought of England as something special, and yet it seemed it had now disowned us. I thought of some mysterious, red-tabbed man in Whitehall who had determined at the stroke of a pen that twenty thousand men should leave this country. So much is fate. There is no way we can avoid it. We had to do as we were instructed, and that was the end of it.

Our ship was called the *Borinquen*, an American ship. It was about fourteen thousand tons, a not very large coastal liner type of craft. It had a passenger capacity of 200 and prior to the war ran tourists down the coast from New York to South America. There were 2,000 of us crammed into this ship, and we were allocated our space. Apparently the vessel had been turned around very quickly as it had arrived with a great cargo of eggs. But the powers that be were in such a hurry to get us away that the ship left England without unloading the cargo, and we were fed buckets of eggs. Any man could have had a dozen eggs at a time had he so desired. On board we got our first sight of big packets of ice cream, all multi-flavored. Our menus featured these two items in abundance, so our cooks were not overstrained.

We set off, sailing due west for days, and I thought, "Oh, we're lucky, we're going to America." But no, apparently we were avoiding the German U-boats. We started to turn south to the Bay of Biscay, into churning waters. The sea became extremely rough: one minute you were climbing a mountain on the deck and the next running down into a canyon.

On board ship the usual social distinction prevailed. Officers used the original dining room, which had been left untouched, and were served at separate tables by white-coated waiters. We were fed at a long table, standing up all the time as there was nowhere to sit, in a place level with the waterline. Suddenly, the sea would swoosh up over the porthole and then recede, a bit disconcerting as we had not yet got our sea legs, but fortunately, I did manage to avoid getting seasick.

One memorable meal consisted of cold pork. We started at one end of the table, and as chaps finished at the other end, we slowly moved along, eating our meal as we went, which allowed newcomers to get their meal at the starting point. It was a human conveyer belt.

In the reception part of the ship where passengers first came aboard was a piano around which we sang, mostly in the evening, in a fog of cigarette smoke. The padre with us used to say, "Well, it won't matter if we get torpedoed. There's no hope for us, so we might as well enjoy ourselves."

We had to man the anti-aircraft guns at night, so we didn't have much time to sleep. When we did we slept in bunk beds, incredibly packed in, and there was no ventilation other than the ship's internal system. No portholes were allowed open, and of course we weren't allowed to show any light. Mostly our quarters were a haze of cigarette smoke.

We stopped at Freetown on the African Gold Coast for a few days but were not allowed on shore. Without fail a tropical storm blew in every night with torrential rain, and we clustered naked on the decks, although the rain was quite warm and not all that refreshing. One night in the hotter parts of the south Atlantic, we watched dolphins, flying fish, and luminescent phosphorescence on the water, shimmering gold and blue—a most wonderful experience I wouldn't have missed.

One evening at teatime, we had frozen fruit from the ship's refrigerator. I had a frozen apple. I awoke in the night and looked around. All the closely packed bunks were empty. Everybody had gone, and I was alone. What had happened? Was I the last man on a sinking ship? Suddenly I knew. Stomach cramps. Every one of us had dysentery.

There were three toilets for about two hundred of us on that deck, which was totally inadequate in this situation. Chaps were leaning over the side letting go, and the corridors were awash. The stench was overpowering. The doctor toiled valiantly, distributing tablets to the lot of us.

When we were recovered, a chap called Rispin who hailed from Blackpool felt we needed compensation. He was a cheeky fellow, enterprising, always looking for adventure. He would barge into the galley, take a joint of meat, and carry it out as if he were on some errand. Nobody ever stopped him, and we would sit there munching the stolen food. On this day he walked into the galley, bold as brass, and picked up a huge tin. The label looked as though it contained plums. He came back with his loot, and we forced open the tin. There filled to the brim was beet root. So much for the good fruit we'd been anticipating. The only thing to do was surreptitiously sling the lot overboard at night. The sea must have turned red. We even had a friendly shark following the ship for miles.

Every night all the accumulated rubbish and garbage from the day would be thrown overboard so that submarines, if any should be about, could not follow the trail. By daylight the mess on the sea would be scattered and well away from where we were.

Our huge convoy, complete with battleships and destroyers—probably thirty or forty ships—would take evasive action and zigzag at certain prearranged times, day and night, without ships crashing into one another. It seemed a masterpiece of organization to me.

Such a great number of troops on board ship must be kept occupied, so each man was given a great lump of blanco. This we were told to daub on our webbing equipment. We didn't take very kindly to this enforced activity, so everybody as one man threw his blanco into the ocean. This time we must have dyed the sea green. Nothing was ever said. Our restlessness in being locked in a ship for a full month, crammed like sardines, was no joke, so it was well-meant to try to keep us occupied but not very successful.

We devised a more pleasant way of passing time. We played a game we called housey-housey (bingo). I had the job of collecting money and handing it to the banker, but a little bit of larceny in my soul prompted me to secrete about ten percent of the takings before handing them over. It was quite a lucrative endeavor.

We met calm waters in the southern Atlantic. If you could ignore the discomfort it was almost like a cruise. We stayed up one night to see St. Helena as we passed by and thought of poor old Napoleon exiled there. Then we pulled into Capetown one morning, and I could see Table Mountain, so aptly named, with its attendant cloud. The sun rose blood red and dyed the sea crimson. Everybody was on one side of the ship watching the coast, causing a thirty-degree tilt to the vessel.

We disembarked at Capetown, and there seemed to be thousands of people waiting to welcome us, some of them German spies, perhaps. Larry and I went ashore and spent five days exploring the town. Lights were blazing, with no blackout there. We went into a restaurant and treated ourselves to steak and chips. People were very receptive, but our stay was too short to become really familiar. We took short journeys on trains and traveled to Simonstown one night, a major area for the fleet. But what stood out so markedly was the apartheid. There were benches for whites only; toilets for whites; cinemas, no blacks; certain sections of buses and trains, no blacks allowed. It hit us hard to see how bad it was.

While we were there, the Queen Mary docked, full of Australian troops, and they were let loose in the town. They were like young animals released from a cage, full of devilment and high spirits. One prank they played was to swap all the babies in prams parked outside the shops. Their idea of fun. The mothers were going berserk. That's what happens when you get chaps released from confining situations. They've got to let off steam.

While in Capetown our colonel complained about the conditions we'd had to put up with on the ship, so we were transferred to another, a British ship called *The Monarch of Bermuda*, a much larger ship. We had rather improved conditions, but there were still some poor devils who had to sleep in the bowels of the ship. It must have been insufferable.

It had taken us a month to reach Capetown, and after our brief sojourn there, we were at sea again. We settled in our new ship (which was torpedoed later on in the war) and were assigned to the anti-aircraft guns on a steel platform protruding over the main deck. Had we slipped we wouldn't have stood a dog's chance of saving ourselves from falling into the ocean, but looking skyward at night we saw the wonderful Southern Cross, the constellations. The air was so clear you could almost touch the stars. It was a good period, then another month at sea before we reached Egypt. The next chapter of my odyssey was beginning.

Chapter 2

Africa, the Desert War

We arrived at Aden on the approaches of the Red Sea and waited there. Native women were busy carrying huge bags of coal on their backs, walking up the gangplanks of the various ships there. We had to wait our turn in line with other ships, and with a barrage balloon attached to our ship we crawled up the Red Sea.

It was July and absolutely oven hot. We'd have a drink of tea, and immediately the perspiration would pour off our backs. Our kidneys had no work to do at all. The fresh water supply was totally inadequate for the vast number of troops who were on board and was severely rationed, but there was a faucet on deck which had a faulty washer and just trickled water. We queued up for hours to get a few dribbles in our cans. We washed in saltwater showers, which produced boils on the skin, and used saltwater soap, which was supposed to lather but never did.

We finally arrived at the start of the Suez Canal at a place called Port Taufiq and went ashore on huge rafts manned by Arabs. While we were on the raft, at a certain time all the Arabs on board suddenly bowed down towards Mecca and started to pray, letting us drift around for a while.

We made land and entered a huge tented camp. Millions of flies were there to greet us, aggressive, persistent. We all immediately developed "jippy tummy," as it was called. Dysentery, really. There was a so-called cinema there, named, for whatever reason, Shafto's, the screen a whitewashed wall. Some of the films were lousy. We were able to buy cans of beer from the NAAFI (Navy, Army, and Air Force Institution), and if it was a film we didn't like, the discriminating audience would show their displeasure by flinging beer cans at the screen. What a clatter! During love scenes chaps would make rather rude sounds; I believe it was because they brought back thoughts of home and loved ones. They didn't want to think of such things.

We were at that camp for two weeks, getting acclimatized. We had no equipment as yet; the guns had gone by another convoy. When they arrived we had to paint them all a yellow, sand color in an effort at camouflage. I doubt it made them all that invisible.

A bit of history in a nutshell may be in order here. Before the war British troops were stationed in Egypt, Italian troops in Libya. When Italy entered the war, fighting broke out on a small scale between these opposing armies. The Italian army was routed at the Battle of Beda Fomm, but then the German army with their formidable General Rommel arrived. We were forced to withdraw to the Egyptian border. We then attacked near Tobruk, and an enormous tank battle ensued in an area called The Cauldron (the Battle of Knightsbridge). We were overwhelmed and forced to retreat to el Alamein.

So at this time there was a terrific uproar. Rommel was crashing on towards Cairo, and there in his way was this bottleneck called el Alamein, where on the northern end was the sea and on the southern end was the Qattara depression: an area of quicksand and salt marshes not even laden camels could traverse, thus impassable by vehicles. It was a better area to defend as Rommel couldn't get around the side of us.

Our chaps who were already there were hard pressed, and we were hurriedly moved up to fill the gap. We had thirty or forty miles to go to the front, and it suddenly hit us. This is it. This is what we've been trained for. This is why the country has spent large sums of money on us. Now we're having to pay our debt. We were really going to be soldiers instead of playing. It took us one or two days to get there, and the general mood was apprehensive.

We were out in the desert, an experience totally new to us, and we wondered, each one of us. In many ways a soldier is a lonely person. He's not able to tell his friends his real inner thoughts; he's not able to show any anxiety. He realizes we're all dependent on each other. We've got to do the job and not let anybody down. This is the thing that keeps you going, not to be seen to be a coward or to do anything foolish. I wondered, how I would react. Would I be able to stand it? I think in your mind it was sometimes rather worse than it turned out to be.

We got to el Alamein and were pushed behind a bank at el Alamein station. It was a station comprised of one small hut, but it was the place of a great battle that was to happen in the future. On arrival we had no idea what to do. Everything and everybody seemed at sixes and sevens. The whole line was in complete chaos. Our troops had retreated so hurriedly that nothing at all had been established.

We were ordered to make an attack to halt the Germans. A hussar regiment, which had previously been provisioned, was at the station. They had their horses with them and were all swagger and derring-do. They also had Honey tanks, small American-made tanks which were rather fast and needed to be. The observation officer of our regiment who was to observe targets for us was in one of these tanks. There were about seventy of them, and they were ordered to attack. Fortunately for our observation officer, his own driver had been taken ill, and a chap who had been in the desert for some time, an old veteran, was assigned to him.

The tanks started out all in line like the Charge of the Light Brigade, pennants flying from the aerials. Everybody was cheering and shouting tally-ho as if they were on a fox hunt. It all seemed so foolish. Then they saw approaching three German tanks, huge things, and what did our chaps do? All in a line they charged. Then the Germans did a strange thing. They ran away.

They ran away, and they ran through a gap they knew of in a minefield that they'd laid. Our chaps ran slap-bang into the minefield. Tanks were blowing up left and right. And behind the minefield was a row of German anti-tank guns. I could imagine the German commander saying, "This is really unfair, chaps. This is too easy."

All hell broke loose. Most of what remained of the seventy tanks, stationary now, were picked off like targets in a fair booth: enveloped in flames, destroyed. We learned a lesson then which we never forgot. We were naive, tricked by the enemy. About ten tanks came back. In one was our observation officer whose driver had not driven in a straight line screaming tally-ho but had zigzagged about and stayed at the back. As soon as he saw what was happening, he sensibly retreated.

We had received no instructions, nothing. There we were, and this great lesson was learned in about half an hour. In the mayhem much of that regiment had disappeared in no time at all, slaughtered. This is what peacetime training does in relation to how you should approach the real thing. It never took into consideration what the other side would do, as if they'd be predictable. Now we knew.

So there we were, well beaten at el Alamein [the Battle of Alam el Halfa], but by this time, General Rommel's troops were strained and needed a rest, his supply lines by then hundreds of miles long, so a kind of stalemate set in.

As we waited, preparing for the fray, our cook opened up his cooking area, and one day we were all queuing at the table for our dinner, the inevitable stew, of course. There were supposedly slices of melon on the table, but the melons could not be seen for flies. A living mass covered them completely. So when we got to dessert, we'd have to attempt to knock off the crawling legions and compete for the fruit.

We had just received our ration of stew, a sergeant, Larry, me, and a couple of other chaps, when a naughty German in a fighter-bomber came over, very inconsiderate of him in the middle of our meal, and dropped some light bombs. We all dived under the nearest vehicle, which happened to be the ammunition truck. As I was lying there I looked sideways and saw a bomb land some thirty yards away with an almighty crash. I suddenly felt hot fluid on my arm. "My God, I've been hit!" I cried. After the raid we scrambled out and then saw that the sergeant had spilled his stew all over my arm. What he called me doesn't bear repeating. It reminded me of a parent who suddenly finds a lost child and in the first relieved instant can only bawl at him.

We had our fixed positions now and bedded and dug ourselves in. Things gradually began to get organized. Prime Minister Winston Churchill came out, and there was to be a change of generalship. He appointed a general named Gott, so-called Strafer Gott, to take over command. General Gott's plane was shot down as he flew back to Cairo from the forward area a few days later. He survived but was killed by machine-gun fire while attempting to rescue others from the wreckage. Consequently, Churchill tapped then General Montgomery for the job, an egocentric man with a high, dominant voice, a man who wouldn't consider any alternative but that we were going to win. He sent out messages that we would stay where we were, that we would not retreat, which had been our way of thinking. And this was a positive statement. This was where we were going to take a stand. We would hold our ground whatever happened.

He drew up plans for the Battle of el Alamein and demanded hundreds and hundreds more tanks and guns. He was determined that he wouldn't submit to pressure to make a move by Prime Minister Churchill. Months were going by, but Montgomery refused to do anything until he got all that he felt he needed.

The Germans made several tentative attacks. We dug an observation post at a place called Ruweisat Ridge, facing south. It took us three days to dig a hole. The ground was solid layers of granite. We used pickaxes, crowbars, hammers, and we had to work during the night as it was rather dangerous to be seen in the open by day. It was an observation post for the expected attack Rommel was going to make around the south end. We thought it rather foolish of him because we felt it was impassable. We had information that the attack was going to come rather quickly, so the observation officer drove up in a tank during the night and left it behind the ridge, out of sight. Cables were led to the dugout, and we put camel scrub around it to hide its obvious nature. The telephone system was run from a trench to the tank and then relayed back to the guns.

There was nothing to be seen up until now. Then one day, under surveillance a mass of German equipment, trucks, and vehicles appeared. The anticipated attack started that night. I was with my crew on the gun, using instruments to correct the firing. During a lull I had to take some rations to the observation post. What a wonderful sight I beheld there. The Royal Air Force was bombing the hell out of the Germans who were trying to get around the south end and had become bogged down. The operation lasted four days, and the RAF did a valiant job. The Germans must have had a terrible time. They had to retreat, and that was the end of Rommel's effort to get through to Cairo.

The huge buildup continued. Infantry divisions came, the Highland Division and the Newcastle-on-Tyne Tees Division, Canadians, Australians, the New Zealanders, South Africans, Indians. We really were a Commonwealth, an Empire Army. Still Montgomery wouldn't move until we were all reinforced and strengthened and given our instructions.

The plan was given to the generals in charge of the divisions, and a few days before the battle commenced we were ordered to go down south to the bottom of the line, right in the middle of the desert, and wait there. Suddenly from out of nowhere, a crowd of natives came, with lots of paraphernalia, looking like a moving fairground. They set up fake vehicles and guns made out of wood and canvas. They were all over the place, hundreds of them. One could have seen they were fakes, but the advantage of it was when the enemy reconnaissance planes came over, taking photographs. They would come over in the early morning and just before sunset. The idea was that the photographs would show shadows and not the actual fake vehicle itself, and they would interpret the photographs from the shadows cast. When we were told to move to the north, where the actual battle would begin, the natives were then ordered to brush our telltale tracks out of the sand, leading the Germans to assume, presumably, that we were about to attack from the south. This was sheer deception, deliberately laid on, but whether or not this ruse ever deceived the enemy was debatable.

Our buildup gave the Germans from May until October to prepare their own defenses. They laid down a huge minefield about a mile deep, thousands of mines in the ground, as the first line of protection. Behind that was a crest which shielded them, and we had to rise onto this crest to make the first attack. This was to be our great effort to break out and throw the Germans back.

Our gun crew had been issued with 600 shells. They were twenty-five pounders, four to a tin, and we pulled them off the ammunition wagons, setting on the firing charges. One hundred pounds each lot weighed; we had aching arms by the time we'd finished our task. We then had to uncap each shell, screw off the metal cap over the firing pin at the front, and then pile them up in readiness.

The time of our attack drew nearer, and we were moved up. The barrage was due to start at ten o'clock that night. Thousands of vehicles were on the move with 1,000 guns lined the full length of the front. This was the number stated. By nightfall we had our ammunition, hundreds and hundreds of shells piled up. It was pitch-black with no moon, and we had to follow prearranged signs to our required position.

We were in columns, and these signs were lit-from-within inverted petrol cans cut out with various signs, such as a circle, new moon, or triangle. With so many men on the move, they had to be kept in the right channels; otherwise, they would have merged and there would have been complete chaos. By following your designated sign, you knew you were in the right lane.

The sand was ground into fine powder, the air full of this dust churned up by heavy vehicles. We were coated with it, our faces, eyes, ears, and noses, and the sweat congealed it almost like concrete. The air was filled with petrol and exhaust fumes, and tanks bellowed out huge plumes of smoke. We tried covering our faces, without much success.

A few of the guns were firing a desultory shell now and then, to deceive the Germans that nothing big was about to happen. Of course they would hear the noise of all these tanks and vehicles, and I doubt they were deceived because they had their spies around our area as we had ours around theirs.

Then it became strangely quiet. Dust hung in the air like fog. All watches were synchronized. Promptly at ten o'clock the order was given. The sergeants screamed "Fire," and we all fired in unison, 1,000 big guns. The night exploded in fury. All hell was let loose. The din, the smoke, the belching flames from the guns, huge flames erupting from the end of the gun nozzle—it was Dante's inferno writ large.

The Germans were all ready for this assault. Heavy forces of German aircraft were coming over and dropping bombs. One bomb hit what was either an ammunition or petrol vehicle. A huge flame shot up, and the fire burned for hours, so the Germans used this as an aiming point.

The din from the guns and bombs was incessant, and we worked as automatons. As a gun layer, I was the person who fired the gun, and my right ear was no more than twelve inches from the barrel. The breechblock dropped, and the sergeant pushed in and rammed the shell home, forced in a charge behind it, and lifted the breechblock to its firing position. He then tapped me on the shoulder to signify it was ready to fire. I laid the gun on its parallel line and pulled the firing bar. The gun reared up like a young stallion and came down with a crash with every shell fired. I then re-laid the gun on its correct line with instruments. We could do this every eight or ten seconds.

This terrible night went on, the smoke, the big guns barking away, smaller guns cracking away, flames illuminating the darkness all along a twenty- to thirty-mile front.

The German anti-tank guns were firing solid steel shells, which could penetrate any tank. One officer, a captain, had come to join us just before the battle started. One of the anti-tank shells came screaming over, missed a tank, and hit him. His stay was brief, about four hours.

We fired all night. I became dizzy, almost like a drunken men. I wasn't even aware that the Germans were firing back at us. I wasn't aware of anything. If you could imagine hell, this was it. I went through the motions like a robot. All the training determined that I would, even though I was in the midst of all this terrible distraction and noise and flame. It was simply manipulating, automatically, without thinking what harm I might be doing. I think my brain had ceased to function as I was going through the motions of firing again and again, hour after hour. In the early hours of the morning my nose was bleeding, and blood was coming from my ears.

German planes came over, dropping parachute flares which gave off an unearthly brilliant yellow light as they floated to earth, a macabre touch to this carnage.

A Canadian anti-aircraft gun was about twenty or thirty yards to the left of us, and even above the mayhem we could hear the sergeant bellowing to the gunners to keep firing at the German aircraft. A bomb scored a direct hit on the gun, and the screaming of the sergeant suddenly ceased. All that was left was a piece of scrap metal that looked as if it belonged in a breaker's yard.

The attack group went in, poor devils. The engineers had to clear a way through the vast German minefield. Somehow or other they disposed of mines and forged a path by laying white tapes showing a safe lane for the infantry and tanks. Our tanks went through. The Germans were waiting. They were solid, well prepared, and our tanks were in trouble on the ridge. Many were ablaze, rows of them on fire, like a long, gigantic gas jet flaring in the night.

When dawn came, smoky and gray, we had to rest. It was more than we could humanly stand. The remaining tanks had to retreat, soundly beaten. The

Germans just sat there. How they'd survived the horrendous shelling, we never knew. They must have been so well prepared, so well dug in.

Our instructions had been to act as a battering ram and force a way through, as there was no way to get around either end. Australian troops and New Zealanders had tried to break through between the sea and the north end of the line and had suffered appalling casualties.

We had to pause. It was impossible. Montgomery had quite rightly laid his plans, but it meant a long battle because we were never going to break through as quickly as all that. But he had a caravan twenty miles or so behind the lines and slept the sleep of the just while all these horrendous happenings were taking place. And rightly so. There was nothing he could do once the plan had gone into effect. He'd told each divisional general precisely what was required, but he couldn't take into account what the Germans would do. Often complete chaos ensues, and instant judgment and action of individuals determine the outcome, regardless of what generals demand. It's removed from authoritarian hands and is left to the man on the ground because the best-laid plans don't always work as specified.

The following morning things had calmed down. Squadrons of RAF planes came over and bombed the German supply lines so that they were left with very little. But we hadn't destroyed the enemy as we had hoped, and Montgomery was hell-bent on bursting a way through their lines, as there was no way around the edges. We'd got to force a direct way through somehow. It was murderous, and the initial assault had been a failure. For ten days this terrible battle went on. We were incurring heavy casualties because as attackers we were suffering greater than the defenders who can often defend an area with very few people. We had thrown all we'd got against the enemy, and Rommel had defended brilliantly.

We hammered at their line, first to the north and then to the south, and on the eighth day, loaded with fresh shells, we prepared for another great battle, one designed to finally break through the German line. God knows what would have happened had it not succeeded.

From a far distance we could hear the wail of the bagpipes of the Fifty-first Highland Division. What an eerie sound over the open desert, like a lament. I suppose it stirred and boosted the morale of the Scottish troops.

Now all was ready for a repeat of what had gone before. In the evening it started, and the great punch had got to go through the middle. I think we'd persuaded Rommel that we might be trying to get through at each end, futile as this might be. We fired and fired, and the night became a pandemonium of noise, smoke, fumes, and flame.

As we were firing, some panic crept in that the Germans had broken through and that we were ordered to retreat. We started to go back when some high-ranking officer appeared, wielding his revolver and threatening to shoot us if we didn't return to our original position. The chaos and the noise around us was like a great orchestra of doom, awe inspiring in a demonic sense, Wagner's *Gotterdammerung*, this officer the conductor, waving his revolver like a baton. Hell on earth.

The final assault went in, and the Germans became fragmented. We had broken through. In their retreat, the Germans left the Italians to their fate by taking their transport vehicles with them.

In the morning we had finished a round of firing, and we were all sitting around the gun completely worn out. I was sitting with my hand on the trail of the gun, and suddenly it was as if a huge hammer had slammed into my hand. I saw blood there and had a bit of a shock not knowing quite what had happened. I was bundled back to the regimental doctor who bandaged me up and said, "We'd better send you back." I think he took pity on me, deciding to give me a rest.

I was sent to a CCS (Casualty Clearing Station), which is the first port of call for wounded people so they can be assessed and patched up, if possible. Amputations also took place there.

This CCS was a huge cavern dug underground behind the lines at el Alamein, and without exaggeration, there must have been about a thousand men in there. It was not a scene for the fainthearted. Numerous doctors had brown rubber aprons on, and they looked as though they were working in an abattoir. There was blood all over the place, chaps crying, screaming, moaning, and every sound of distress you could imagine. My wound was so trivial I had to wait while other poor devils were either being patched up and sent away to hospitals further down the line or laid on one side ready for burial. A few hours later I was attended to. A probe was put through the hole left by the shrapnel, and I was bandaged up again. I was sent off and finished up in an ambulance with other wounded. The ambulance reeked with the sweet smell of blood; it was so sickly, sticky, one could almost eat the atmosphere. The vehicle jolted and bumped over the rough, uneven track, and these poor souls were thrown around, screaming aloud in their agony. For good measure, the Germans dropped a few bombs off to the side of us. I don't think they were really aiming at us but just wanted to make things more unpleasant.

I finished up in a hospital in Alexandria. I was there for a couple of days and then went to a depot where I had to report to get back to my unit. It was manned by South African personnel, not very pleasant chaps, and whenever they saw me they started to speak in Afrikaans. I was pleased when a vehicle from the regiment came to pick me up, and back I went. When I returned to my unit, the Battle of el Alamein was just about over.

I realized then that my next of kin would have been informed by telegram that I'd been wounded, with no clarification as to whether it was a minor wound or major amputation. It brought home to me how relatives, parents and wives, had to live with uncertainty month after month, reading and hearing news but not knowing what was happening to their son or husband.

I hurriedly wrote an airgraph to my wife, telling her what a trivial wound it was, to set her mind at rest, but the period of time she had to wait between the telegram and my letter must have been pretty difficult.

Letters were the thing that kept us going. Delivery of mail, erratic as it was, especially in the middle of battle, was vital. We would get nothing for long periods and then three or four letters all at once. This contact with home saved us from going crazy, giving us hope that one day it would be over, no matter how impossible, how uncertain that dream seemed now.

Now that we had broken through, there came the great logistics problem of keeping supplies moving and replacing casualties and vehicles that had been destroyed. Only a limited number of forces was allowed to advance and chase the Germans. The entire front couldn't move off in one block and continue the chase. A lot of reorganization had to take place. It's surprising how much fuel a division uses; thirty thousand gallons of petrol a day and food and ammunition had to be constantly supplied.

We moved so far, and then the rains came. It poured, and the desert became waterlogged because a lot of it isn't sand; it's granite and other rock. So we had an enforced respite and waited. The desert suddenly bloomed. Millions of tiny flowers appeared, orange, red, blue, purple, a riot of color, a pointillist painting. But their life-cycle was short. After a few hours they died.

As we waited we organized ourselves. Our rations came up in a sack with rice, cheese, tinned butter and bacon, and biscuits. Bread we would occasionally get, but it was usually green, damp, and rotten.

One chap hit on the idea of making a rice pudding in a dish using water and rice with perhaps a little milk. He was preparing it when a sandstorm blew up. We saw it approaching like a black thunder cloud, and then it hit us. Quickly, we scrambled into the vehicles and closed the windows against the gale and sand swirling around us. The rice pudding unfortunately received an inch-thick covering of sand. We scraped it off and ate the rest of the pudding. Rice and sand proved to be an excellent purgative.

Eventually, we were ready to be on the move again. Slowly, tentatively at first, as the enemy withdrew, we advanced westwards. We engaged in many skirmishes as we continued our advance. We'd hit the Germans and fight until it got dark, and then by common agreement, it seemed, both sides ceased for the night. The enemy would be on one side of a hill, and a few miles away we'd be on the other. We'd bed down and form a *laager*, a square with tanks and guns on the outside and soft vehicles in the middle, and we would have a relatively quiet night. During that time the Germans would put out a protective screen while the rest of them retreated.

We came across an abandoned, heavily damaged German gun in a gun pit. There was little left as those who had survived had departed, except that in one corner lay a camouflage net, rolled up. We disturbed this net, and a million flies flew out, and when we unrolled it there were the remains of a German soldier. My stomach turned at the sight. It wasn't a whole person, just pieces.

We reached el Adem, south of Tobruk. Wrecked German planes were scattered on the ground at the airfield at Gambut. There we were suddenly transferred to the Seventh Armored Division, the old Desert Rat division which had been in Africa since 1939. We were joining the real veterans. We replaced a regiment whose guns were worn out. So we became desert rats and started on a new adventure.

We'd set off first thing in the morning and inevitably run slap-bang into the enemy, and sometimes it took the rest of that day to break through. We reached the furthest point west than we'd ever been before, a place called el Agheila, and it was similar to el Alamein inasmuch as it was all salt marsh and with only a narrow, solid bottleneck.

In previous advances, our forces had got that far and had then been beaten back. They'd been fighting the Italians in the early campaign, and they'd proved not too difficult to deal with. Although in many cases the Italians did fight very well, I think their heart was not in it. You've got to have a reason; otherwise, you're no good at all. By then, of course, the Germans had arrived in large numbers with the great desert fox, General Rommel, at their head. He was a real canny adversary.

About this time we found a live chicken. Where it came from was a mystery. We called it Daisy, and it became very tame. It was our chicken, our mascot, our lucky charm, and we became very fond of it. We had a little metal locker in the back of the vehicle, and we used this as a hutch for Daisy. It had a small door, and as the bird would have suffocated without air, we rigged a piece of wire so that the door remained open just a couple of inches. We used to let her out when we made a stop, then when we called her she would come back like a trained dog and scuttle into her hutch. When sandstorms hit, the chicken would crouch under the vehicle, braving the sand and wind that was like a blast of air from an oven. So Daisy travelled along with us, head sticking out of the partly open door, feathers fluttering. One day something wonderful happened. Daisy laid an egg!

We were delayed at el Agheila for some time waiting for reinforcements to come up. We were stranded, sinking into the salt marsh, and the engineers had to bring up pontoons of some sort so that our vehicles could get across. At the precise time we were trying to get across, the Germans came and rather disturbed us with a bombing raid. It was very unpleasant; there we were, stuck in this salt marsh with nowhere to go. We just had to stand by, pray, and hope for the best.

We finally got through and went even further west. Nobody had any maps; the country was completely alien to us. We were south of the line, deep in the desert. The Australians were north near the sea, as was the Fifty-first Highland Division, which we felt was a better place to be. We were always left down on the south edge, about thirty miles from the sea, and by looking at the sky you could place its location because the sky, instead of being a yellowy, misty haze, was a bright blue there.

We had little time to eat anything during the day, but we devised a wonderful method of brewing tea in a hurry. We kept our tea stored in thick iron cans in lockers in the vehicles, and these were red with rust, but it made no difference to us. Often we'd stop because of some obstruction in the way, maybe for only a few minutes. Then we pulled out an empty four-gallon petrol can, a very thin, blackened tin, which we'd cut in half so that it was about a foot high and twelve inches square. The bottom half we used as a fire tray. We dumped sand in the tray, poured petrol into the sand, and ignited it. For our tea we had a round tin with a handle, which had once held potatoes and which held about a gallon of water. We lowered the pan of water over the flaming sand with a bayonet and poured "compo tea" in. That was tea, powdered milk, and sugar mixed together. The mixture boiled almost in seconds, sending up a head of foam. It never tasted like tea really, but it was something deeply ingrained in us to make a mug of tea. As we were briefly halted we could see the long line of vehicles, all with these blazing tins. What a wonderful sight it was! We perfected this ritual to within two or three minutes at the most; we had to because we were always in a hurry. Officers were part and parcel of this ritual, too. They wanted their mug of tea as well.

Suddenly we'd get the order to move off, and all we had to do was lift up the tea can, throw out the residue, kick the flaming contents of the pan into the sand, and hook both pans onto our vehicle. We were like a gypsy caravan with tins clanging all over the place. But we were very organized; everybody had a specific job to do, so the operation was most efficiently run.

When we were on active service, of course, we had to feed ourselves. It was only when we were stationary for any length of time that the cook could set up his cookhouse. A very peculiar character was our cook, someone you never wished to fall out with because you'd get short rations. We had oblong mess tins with a folding handle and a mug. Food was slopped into the tin and accompanied by hot tea, manna from heaven for us. Otherwise, we had our own rations. They came up in boxes, mostly from America or Australia. Rations were for fifteen men for one day or for one man for fifteen days. The mathematics were brilliant.

The quartermaster who issued these rations kept the case containing steak and kidney puddings for himself, so we rarely got these until he became so sick and tired of them, he'd issue them to us. Our staple diet was stew and bully beef, very good, but we did get fed up with the same old menu. Our ration boxes also contained a few sweets, cigarettes, and everything else that was necessary, Nothing was forgotten; even toilet paper was included.

We were dealing with a cunning enemy. German aircraft dropped fake bars of chocolate and fountain pens. You picked one up, and it would blow up and you'd lose your hand. Of course this was effective only for so long, until we got wise to the event, but this was the sort of trick that was played. It was always a cat and mouse situation. The enemy laid land mines all over the place, and our engineers went along with bayonets, prodded the ground at an acute angle, and lifted them. So what the enemy did was to extend a wire beneath the surface mine to one lower down, and as the engineer lifted the mine, that set off the one below. That was the end of the engineer. We eventually got wise to that ploy. Then the enemy started to make mines of wood so that the mine detectors were ineffective. And so it went on, a pretty lethal game.

The Germans also devised a novel way of bombing. They would send over two or three light fighters, each equipped with a couple of bombs, hundred pounders. Instead of bombing in the conventional way, they came in at virtually ground level, causing the bombs to skim along the surface of the ground like pinballs. One day we happened to be on the outside of a group of vehicles scattered all over the place. Some chaps were eating in the back of a vehicle when an enemy aircraft appeared, flying low, and released a bomb, which came skidding along and smashed right into it. There was an almighty crash, and all that remained was bits of metal, no trace of bodies.

All I could think of was yet another handful of official telegrams dispatched, regretting the death of . . . your husband . . . son.

The Germans also knew how to play psychological warfare. Many of their Stuka dive-bombers had loud whistles attached to them, and for us on the ground the effect on one's nerves was horrendous. The bomb itself also had a whistle attached to it, and it seemed as though every bomb was aimed for the back of your neck. Such devices were indeed shattering to the nervous system.

One all-pervasive problem we had was the flies. We would move to a virgin area of desert with not a fly in sight. Five minutes later there would be a million, those we had brought with us and who knows how the rest had found us. They swarmed everywhere, clustering on the sides of the mouth and eyes, impossible to swat away. We had enamel mugs which we attached to our belts and which held about a pint of tea. We would sit in our vehicle with our filled mugs, and a hundred or more flies would settle on the rim, their proboscides busy, searching for moisture. We would flap them away and take a quick gulp of tea as they rose in a cloud and then swooped right back like a bunch of dive-bombers. All day long they would pester us, but as soon as the sun went down, they all disappeared. Lord knows where they hid, but as soon as the sun rose, there they were, the swarming legions.

During the day, temperatures would reach a shimmering 120 degrees Fahrenheit, and at night it would drop below freezing. We wrapped scarves around our stomachs then, to prevent trouble, as we developed severe stomach pains unless we were very careful.

Another problem that was rarely mentioned, but one that affected thousands of men in the Western Desert, was that of sanitation. We were constantly on the move and had no sanitation facilities at all. When we had the call of nature, we would take a shovel, go out about twenty paces from where the vehicle was, dig a slight hole to just scrape the surface, bend down, and do what we had to do, then scrape earth back, rather like a cat. Of course with two hundred thousand men doing that every day, plus urinating, hey presto, it was heaven for flies, helped also by corpses that were often lying around.

Whenever possible we dug pits for our guns. Fairly close to us, but not one of our regiment's, was a twenty-five-pounder gun in a pit. During an air raid a bomb landed right in that pit. There had probably been five or six men in the crew, and when we went to investigate the damage we didn't expect to see anyone alive. By some miracle one survivor was left untouched, but he was stark, raving mad. Within those few minutes he'd gone crazy from shock. No need to describe the scene further. The lone survivor would probably have been better off killed as well.

In action, depending on the urgency of the target, we would get the order to fire "ten rounds rapid." We'd have ten shells ready, each gun, and blast off as hard as we could. There were other occasions when we observed an accumulation of enemy troops, perhaps getting ready to make an attack, and we'd get what we termed a stonk—for no apparent reason, perhaps the sound of the word appealed to us—an accumulation of, say, ten, twenty, or thirty shells at the side of each gun. Then at a given signal we'd fire all of them, perhaps one hundred and twenty shells, as rapidly as possible and bring down a real clatter on the enemy. There were many different ways of organizing an attack.

At nighttime when we fired, there was a terrific flare out of the end of the gun barrel, a good giveaway as to our position. But some charge cases made in Canada had the remarkable ability not to flare when we fired them; just a few sparks came out. We were so intent on safety we would save these special charge cases just for night firing, and for good reason.

Often at night three of us would be detailed to go out to separate points on the compass to spot German artillery firing. We timed a particular flash exactly, and the three of us would take a bearing from our different places. Coming back there would be angles and lines drawn from our position on a map, so that all would lead to one precise point in the apex. So we had a bead on where the German guns were. The only disadvantage was that if they moved afterwards during the night we were wasting our shells on the desert air. But this was one of the ways we tried to pinpoint German artillery, and they were doing the same to us.

A premature burst in the gun was rare but could be extremely dangerous and often fatal. When that happened, the shell, instead of leaving the gun, jammed for some inexplicable reason, probably due to a faulty shell, one slightly not the right shape, as they had to be absolutely accurate in size. It would blow up the barrel of the gun like a balloon. Sometimes with the most dire of consequences the barrel would burst. You can't imagine the energy behind the power of the charge which enables the shell to do its business and come out the other end.

Once when we were going after the Germans, our driver, Broome, was sent back to have a painful toe, some sort of infection, taken care of, and I, who had been given a hasty driving lesson across a hundred yard stretch of sand, was ordered to drive the vehicle. This quad, as it was called—why, I never knew, perhaps because it had four wheels, but so had all the other vehicles—was completely enclosed within thin steel and had sliding windows. If you can imagine a vehicle of that description sitting out in the midday heat of the desert, an oven would be a poor comparison. To cap it all, we often had to keep the windows closed because of the legions of flies. Behind and attached to this vehicle was the gun limber, which carried ammunition, and hooked on that was the gun itself with wheels and a trail. With this caravan we bounced along.

On this particular day, the top of the vehicle was open so that the sergeant in control of the whole contraption could stand on his seat and look out over the vehicle for marauding enemy planes that might strafe with machine-gun fire or bomb. This didn't occur with too much frequency, but when it did, we jumped out of the vehicle as fast as possible and got as far away as we could from the target it presented.

We were travelling along at a fairly good clip, and with my newly learned, albeit sketchy, driving skills, I was my feeling my oats, a racing driver, no less. This feeling came to an abrupt halt when I ran into an unseen pothole. The vehicle shot up and the sergeant shot down. The sky was blue, I recall, but not as blue as the atmosphere inside the vehicle. I finally got us out and on the way again.

Now, on the shield of the gun a leather case was strapped which contained the dial sight. This was the instrument I used for gun laying. It was always kept in the case when we were not in action as it was an expensive and important piece of equipment. A mile or so further along we had to make a stop, and someone noticed the leather case was missing. The sergeant was now even less pleased with the whole expedition. We turned around and fortunately were able to retrace our tracks in the sandy terrain. There against the pothole lay the missing dial sight case, apparently having bounced off when we made our unscheduled halt. There we were, in the middle of the desert, all alone; everybody had gone on ahead. So we kept on, hopefully westward, until we caught up with the main body of our unit. Nobody thanked me for safe deliverance. We were all relieved when Broome returned.

We pulled up at a small oasis. We had to get to our position during the night because there was a big hill in front of us, and somewhere—although we had infantry scouting it, we couldn't determine exactly where—a German observer was up there. We had to work like hell and dig a gun pit as fast as we could. It took five of us all night to complete, having to dig a circular area about fifteen yards in diameter and five feet deep with a ramp in order for the gun to be hauled into the hole. By the next day all was ready.

We were behind palm trees, so we weren't easily visible, but the fact that we were firing gave our position away to the observer. Shells were falling, not too close, probably due to poor aiming, but close enough to cause concern. Suddenly we heard this gun fire, and we followed the shell with our ears every yard of the way from that gun. It landed right on the edge of our gun pit, the outside edge, fortunately, with a colossal bang, like a giant crashing into steel. The bang and pungent smell bought chaps running to see if we were alive. They feared the shell had landed slap in the gun pit itself. It had landed no more than four or five inches on the outside of the pit. Another foot and it would have been smack in the pit itself. It was a fraction short of total disaster and curtains for us. Guardian Angel number two.

After that incident, when the firing started again just off to our left, I shot into my little trench at the side of the pit we'd dug earlier. On top of me tumbled a brigadier, shaking with fear. He begged my pardon and said would I please let him in. A brigadier! I didn't have much choice. So I asked him if he couldn't use his authority to get us out of this place because we'd be in dire trouble if we stayed here much longer. Two or three hours later we did pull out.

There were other dangers in the desert. Our Sergeant Eason was answering a call of nature, and as he was so occupied, a scorpion stung him on his bum. Tough as he was, that laid him out for about three days. Covered in blankets, he lay shivering and shaking and burbling away, no match for a scorpion.

Now and then we were pulled out of action for a short rest, and it was up to us to make what recreation we could. During one of these rest times, someone had the bright idea of getting up a game of cricket. We carried all sorts of stuff with us, and we routed out a bat, stumps and ball, and also a length of matting which we rolled down for the pitch. We were well into the game when play was held up by a camel train crossing the wicket. It was probably the only match in the history of cricket that camels stopped play by traipsing across the pitch!

In case you think it was one round of fun and jokes, it wasn't. But we tried. One day Rispin, Larry, and I were attempting to fry tinned sausages. We found a sort of pan—we had to improvise with most things—and got a fire going. Rispin was our official machine gunner, and as we were sitting there tending our food, a hostile plane came over and started machine gunning. Rispin fired at the plane with his Sten gun, a valiant but futile effort. When we were able to attend to our interrupted cuisine again, there was our frying pan full of cartridge cases, sausages and cartridge cases all mixed up. We sorted them out, and nobody ate a cartridge case.

Rispin was an odd man; he had no defined job at all, and nobody ever bothered him. He wasn't on the guns and was ostensibly our machine gunner, but there was hardly ever need for a machine gun. He had the habit of sleeping under the ammunition truck, a huge steel vehicle carrying all the ammunition, spare shells by the hundreds, and cartridge cases for firing. He used to say, "They won't hit this," but the rest of us didn't share his confidence.

As time went on we all came down with desert sores, mostly on our fore-arms, and everybody seemed to be affected, hundreds and hundreds of men. They were circular sores about half an inch in size, like cones of a volcano, festering, filled with pus. Settled around the edges were the ever-present flies; we couldn't even feel them, but when we looked, there they would be, feeding. We would go to the first-aid post, get a pair of scissors, pull off the crust that had formed, then take a piece of cotton wool on the end of the scissors and scrape out the pus and mess until the pit looked clean. Then we would bandage the whole lot up.

We were called out on parade one day. Some brigadier who probably didn't know we were fighting a war wanted to inspect us. We were all lined up, about a hundred of us, and every single man had his arms bandaged. We must have looked a pathetic lot.

Apparently, the abrasive nature of the sand was responsible for our plight. Even if there were no apparent sand about, it was ingrained in our towels and would act abrasively when we dried ourselves. The wind carried sand, too. It was all-pervasive. This, combined with lack of fresh food, particularly vegetables, was the cause. Everything we had was tinned, not a good diet, but the quality of the food was not bad. What we received from Australia, bacon, butter, cheese, even potatoes, was adequate but inevitably tinned.

Once in the desert I lost my wedding ring. We became so dehydrated we slimmed down considerably, and the ring became loose and slid off somewhere, fortunately while we were stationary. Imagine trying to locate a ring in the desert sand! I scrabbled around my immediate area and, by an incredible stroke of luck, found it. From that day on I wore it on my middle finger. Such a lucky break wouldn't happen twice.

At times the troop movement would become very fluid when we were scrapping with the enemy. During one such period we were all over the place, and so were they. So we were sent out as totally separate guns to see if we could spot any pockets of Germans. We were always glad to get back from these rather silly operations. We were on our own, just one gun, and while we were scratching our bums waiting and wondering what to do, two German planes came over at a few thousand feet. I could almost read the pilots' thoughts. Because the position was so fluid, they didn't know whether we were friend or foe. I had a sudden brain-wave. "Wave to them!" I shouted to the other chaps. "Wave!" So we did, and it seemed to convince them that we were on the right side. They went away without giving us any further trouble.

We were approaching Wadi Zamzam, a huge fissure that had been a water course centuries ago. A steep bank sloped downward, and we had to wait to get people across to see what it was like on the other side. We had been there all day, and the following morning I was sitting and waiting with one of the drivers. We had dug our inevitable slit trenches, one for each of us, rather like digging a grave, only not so deep. We used to joke that it was doubly useful. If anything happened to you, others could just throw you in there and fill you in.

This driver and I were about five or six yards from each other, each sitting on the edge of our own trench with our legs dangling into the hole. The lorry came up with our breakfast, and I offered to go and fetch it. I went to the vehicle and got some bacon and fried bread for both of us and, returning to my spot, gave him his meal, and we started eating the food. Suddenly without warning, not more than ten or fifteen yards in front of us came a thunderous crash and an eruption of black smoke as a huge shell exploded. We hadn't even heard it coming; it must have come in on carpet slippers without any of the normal warning sounds. I reeled against the tremendous blast, the vast movement of air, and ducked down, obviously a bit late. A few seconds later I emerged to find that my companion, unfortunately, had been hit by a large piece of shrapnel which had ripped away the lower part of his face. The ambulance came and removed him but had only gone a few hundred yards before he died. Guardian Angel number three for me at Wadi Zamzam.

Later, thinking about this rogue shell, I concluded that, considering its size, which I could well estimate by this time, it was from a siege gun fired from a great distance. I knew that guns often were left loaded for instant use in an emergency, and this gun had not been needed during the night. Before departure next morning, troops would fire the shell off at random in order to empty the gun. Such are the ironies of war.

Everybody became trigger-happy. One day an RAF plane flew low along the whole gamut of the front line. He must have been in trouble. At the beginning of the line some anti-aircraft gunners had started firing, and all the way down the line this plane was being fired on. Nobody seemed to realize he wasn't the enemy. By the grace of God he was so low that nothing was able to hit him; but it illustrates how trigger-happy everybody became, how badly lacking in judgment men become when their nerves are frayed and on edge.

We saw so many planes shot down, Spitfires shot down, Messerschmidts shot down, wretched planes that had made forced landings, fools practicing low-level bombing or machine gunning. One chap came whizzing down to ground level and hit the Bofors gun, an anti-aircraft gun which had a barrel about six feet long. That was the end of him. We watched such events with total equanimity, without any problem at all.

Much as we depended on each other, even in our circumstances one got tired of the incessant company of other men. We were never out of each other's sight, and we all slept in the same place, under the vehicle at the side of the gun.

So one night I went a few yards away into the desert, put down my bed, and lay there looking at the sky. A moon had risen, and the stars were intense, so low it seemed I could have plucked them.

This might sound rather childish and romantic, but I recall vividly my feeling of loneliness of soul and the sense of the futility and uncertainty of life. Then the thought suddenly came to me that this same moon and stars could be seen by my wife, and I felt that, somehow, there was a bond, a connection between us, although I was a thousand miles away and wondering whether I would ever see England again because the odds were pretty long. I even tried thought transference to get over a message to her that, so far, I was all right. Then common sense took over, and I thought that most likely it was cloudy in England with no visible moon and stars. Even so, that feeling of connection persisted, a small comfort.

We had Christmas before arriving in Tripoli. We were provided for very well, with tinned turkey and a bottle of beer. It was really simplicity itself, but to us it was wonderful. Arrangements were extremely good. I think, too, we had a mobile shower then. It was the only shower I had in the whole campaign! I must have stunk to high heaven. We were so short of water that we resorted to washing our clothes in petrol. We were allowed about a gallon of water a man, and everything had to come out of that, tea for the day, washing, and everything else. It left about a mug of water per person per day to drink.

On Christmas Day, sergeants waited on us before we ate, and—forgive the language—everybody was pissed up on that day. I think by common consent the Germans did the same sort of thing. They felt as we did, and hostilities ceased for that day. So we made what we could of the day, little knowing that it was going to be the last Christmas for some of us.

At the beginning of January 1943, we started the usual advance, facing the Germans early in the morning. It was a gorgeous day. Our normal procedure was to advance as a small spearhead with the main division behind us. We were in the lead. There were about half a dozen tanks, a few infantrymen, probably one or two engineers, and our four guns, which comprised a troop.

Suddenly, we had alarming SOSs from the tanks. They had run into German guns, and we were hurriedly asked to supply support, just the four guns. The area was as flat as a billiard table, and we stopped in all urgency and prepared to start to fire. We could see in the distance a slight hill which seemed to have been causing problems for the tanks. It became clear later that the German guns had been there preparing all night, ready for our early morning advance. We had neither time nor opportunity to dig any holes or trenches for protection in the event of any problem.

We were ordered to fire, which meant that the vehicle towing us brought us onto the flat gun position, unhooked the guns and the ammunition limber, and departed out of the way. We lowered our gun and brought the ammunition down the side and prepared to commence firing. As we were doing this, all was quiet.

As soon as we had dropped the gun and the vehicle had departed, the Germans sent over a shell to get the range, and it landed right where we were. I had a sense of foreboding. I was aware of what that meant. We started to fire. Whether we were anywhere near the target, I don't know. The Germans were there, with guns and tanks, able to see us over open sights; they didn't need anybody to range for them. They had perhaps been ranging before we arrived.

Our four guns fired about two shells each, and then it was absolutely hell. Shells poured down on us, right on us. There was no question of any missing or going over or under or wide. They were all on top of us. We were completely exposed, four guns with six men on each, twenty-four men plus the gun position officer and three other men. There was nothing we could do. We couldn't continue firing; it was beyond even our trained ability to withstand that deadly barrage. All we could do was to lay as flat as possible. We couldn't face the torrent of shells that was crashing all around us. Every shell came to do damage. None of them was wasted.

I crouched low behind the wheel of the gun. The sergeant was in the middle. Shrapnel was screaming all over the place. We weren't stalwart enough to stand up to that onslaught. Life preservation dominated. How long the inferno lasted I don't know. It could have been half an hour, it could have been any time. I was not conscious of anything, not conscious of fear, not conscious of the horrendous damage.

The man next to me on the gun crew, Nobby Clarke—another Nobby Clarke, not my earlier friend—instead of lying flat had kneeled at the side of me. I yelled to him to get down, and then I saw that he was perfectly motionless, his spectacles still on his nose. I suddenly saw blood dripping into the sand. He was rigid, didn't fall over, just kneeled there. He was dead.

Then, I suppose, the Germans ran out of ammunition because the barrage suddenly stopped. One gun had continued to fire, Sergeant Short's, on which was my friend Larry.

The shield of our gun, a quarter inch of steel, was pitted with holes. There was an ambulance on the gun position which was also riddled with shrapnel, and the gun position officer was screaming to the battery major over the telephone to enable us to withdraw. The major was secure in a slit trench further back, and his signaler in a truck at his side was yelling at him to give us permission to withdraw. The major got a military cross for his valour. We did get the order to withdraw.

Now, to see a man who is mortally wounded is not pleasant. You can't recognize him; his face has changed. A bombardier on Sergeant Short's gun, a young, clean-featured man with fair, wavy hair, was dying. His hair had gone dull, lost its luster, and his face was ashen.

We loaded dead and wounded on the bonnet of the vehicles as best we could. One chap we brought back had a huge wound in his leg, and his artery was pumping out blood with every beat of his heart. We laid him on a rubber sheet watching as his heartbeat pumped blood. He suddenly said how cold he was. He called for his mother. Then he died.

We tried to sort ourselves out. All was quiet. We checked who was there. I found that my friend was missing. Larry was not there. So I asked permission to go back and try to find him. I went back and found him. He was sitting on the ground, just sitting, deathly pale. He had a bloody gash in his back, and he asked me for a cigarette. I lit one and gave it to him. He inhaled, and the smoke came out of his back. The ambulance came and took him away. The news came that he'd died that evening at the casualty clearing station. He'd contracted pneumonia. I knew under those circumstances, with the trauma, it makes a man vulnerable to things like that.

I was cut, totally cut. My friend had gone, had dropped away on the long road that was to take us to Berlin. I believe I became an old man then. We all did. How can you adequately describe to anyone how it was, what it was?

Sergeant Short received a military cross for being brave, but it was very foolish. Of his crew, four were killed, the sergeant himself was wounded, and one man was miraculously unscathed. We lost two men on our gun, and in total, fifty percent of the crews died.

No, Sergeant Short wasn't wise. If you learn anything, it's that you live to fight another day. All the dead on his gun were finished; for them the war was over. We could continue to fight the Germans, but his gun was decimated.

I realized then that the Germans were doing a job in the same way that we would have done under similar circumstances. Something else I began to perceive was what we were doing to each other. We spoke a different language, wore different uniforms, were under different authority, and yet we all had a common bond. We were all in it for no reason that we personally were responsible for. I never, ever, during the whole period of the war, hated the German soldiers at all because I quickly learned that they were only doing a job the same as us. Gunner Schmidt was simply my counterpart. We did impose the same horror on them when we caught them in a disadvantageous position and fired on them, and so the equation was about equal.

We were approaching Tripoli and began to see at last slight signs of fertility in the ground, some scrub, slight grass where the desert had not encroached. I saw a small almond tree, I think it was that, a little bush no more than a foot high. I suppose, in a way, by that time I was sick of it all, dog tired, dirty, disheartened. And this poor little tree, struggling against adversity, sand already threatening to smother it, had just one small blossom on it. Such a brave little thing. Suddenly, I felt it was parallel to my own feeling. It was struggling to carry on with no sign of a future. A wealth of sympathy overwhelmed me. I wanted to dig it up and put it in some fertile soil and give it a chance of life. I knew it was doomed. I may have been run down, I may have been depressed, I may have been sentimental, but I gave way to tears.

We had to move on. We thought we were going into Tripoli. It was wonderful to see cultivation, green growing things, palm trees, unbelievable after so may months of desolation. I felt new hope.

We were halted one night on the outskirts of Tripoli and ordered to polish our boots. Polish our boots! We couldn't believe it. Maybe it was because of our dirty boots, but we weren't allowed to stay in Tripoli. Some of the regiments were allowed to stay and had a victory parade. We were ordered to move through Tripoli and carry on and face the Germans. There seemed to be no respite at all.

At times the gun crews got on each other's nerves. What could we talk about? We remarked about this and that, but our main preoccupation was what lay ahead, and what we all wanted, naturally, was eventually to go home.

I'm sure the chaps on the other side felt the same. I thought again of Gunner Schmidt over there, doing exactly what I was doing. He had his problems, his family, his responsibilities, too. He wanted to go home as much as I did. I could almost commiserate with him. What were we doing there in the Western Desert, all of us, Europeans, in this alien land? How incomprehensible it all seemed.

We advanced in stops and starts and reached the Mareth Line—a natural protection of mountains the Germans had prepared very strongly. In the meantime, the First Army had landed in Algiers and was approaching from the other end, so our opponents were squeezed between us and the First Army, composed mostly of Americans and some British.

These troops were extremely new and green, not battle hardened, and although they fought very well, they were not able to capture Tunis. They got very close and were pushed back. The Americans were caught with their tanks in the Kasserine Pass, and I believe it was their first experience of close combat. Unfortunately, they panicked and retreated, leaving their tanks behind. One of the great dilemmas we had in the final stages of the war in Tunis was fighting Germans in

American Sherman tanks. It was a great pity that this happened, primarily because of the inexperience of soldiers.

We battled through the Mareth Line. There was a long, flat plain reaching to the mountains, and the Germans had built a huge ditch as a tank trap. The Fiftieth Tyne Tees Division, men from Newcastle-upon-Tyne, were ordered to attack. They were slaughtered, mown down, and things got so bad that we had to raise a white flag and send ambulances onto the battlefield. The Germans did cease firing while we picked up the dead and wounded. When the ambulances had done their job and departed, the battle began again. We finally overcame the enemy as New Zealanders went round the southern edge and caused the Germans to retreat.

They were now trapped between our Eighth Army and the First Army coming up from the other side, who made a final effort to take Tunis and failed. We were ordered to go around, and we went vast distances overnight and right into the German sector. The German forces must have stood there with their jaws agape at the sight of us. We looked like a gypsy caravan, dirty, scruffy, any sort of headwear, our gear, vehicles, and guns clapped out, ruined after our two-thousand-mile journey across open desert. We were the filthy individuals who had been brought in to make the final push to try and enter Tunis, and we did succeed after a final, terrific battle.

The first troops to enter Tunis found German soldiers still walking around arm-in-arm with local girls. They had had no warning as to how close we were, and after a short skirmish, everything was finished. To all intents and purposes, the battle in Africa was over.

We continued to advance just beyond Tunis and came to a small river. Because we'd advanced so far, we were bombed by RAF fighter bombers. Bombed by our own side! The final irony. Fortunately, no one was killed, and only one of the vehicles suffered damage.

This locale was a mosquito area, and we were issued with a net to put over our face, but it was so hot it made us even more uncomfortable, and we would remove it. We were also given evil-smelling stuff to rub on our skin, which repelled everybody, not just mosquitoes. At about 3 A.M. when we were trying to get some sleep, the effects of this darned ointment wore off and the mosquitoes bit like hell, so we'd wake up in the morning frantic with bites.

We were sent to do some observing with the officers. We had plenty of ammunition and nothing to do with it, really. We reached a ridge that overlooked a road some distance away. There was no movement there, not a thing to be seen. After a while we observed a German vehicle, easily recognizable as we had seen many of them during the course of the war, traveling along this deserted road. Ah! Here was a nice, tasty target.

As we watched, the vehicle stopped, apparently having broken down. We had all this ammunition to waste and nothing better to do, so we started lobbing shells as the lone occupant, a German officer, got out, opened the engine compartment, which was in the rear of those vehicles, peered inside, and fiddled about as our shells were bouncing down, seemingly oblivious to the mayhem going on around him. He apparently eventually found the problem, got back in the vehicle, and drove off. In one sense, watching that man made me feel proud to be a human being. Such aplomb, such coolness under fire. Not many could emulate that. We almost wished him well.

We were ordered to stand down. We were lined up in a field by the side of the road and ordered to clean and polish our guns. There was almost mutiny! Fortunately, common sense took over among the upper echelons, and we were left in peace.

We were moved to a place called Bou Arada, a completely arid spot fifty miles southwest of Tunis. It was in the middle of nowhere, just open desert. To say we were annoyed was to put it mildly. Fortunately, it was a short stay, and we were then sent to a place called Homs on the coast, about sixty miles east of Tripoli. There we rested from May, or thereabouts, until September.

All we had to do, really, during this time, was bathe naked in the sea. The sand was so white it hurt my eyes. In this small township we confiscated a building and turned it into a rest place where we could write, read, or just relax. The NAAFI set up shop so we could get tea and buns. We would spend an hour or so there. It was very small, but it helped.

During this time I was sent out as plenipotentiary to barter with some nearby Arabs. We had bully beef, and they had eggs. I met an Arab who invited me into a tent, and I found these people to be full of courtesy and good manners. Before I was allowed to negotiate anything, I had to sit cross-legged on a carpet facing my host who prepared hot, bitter, stringent coffee. We sipped from small cups. The civility and ritual in such an area of blood and war was wonderful to experience. We decided on an agreement that I would give him so many tins of bully beef, and he would give me so many eggs. The exchange seemed quite fair to me, so we made our farewells, and I went back with the eggs. I felt very satisfied.

The Arabs also wanted tea. They loved tea. After we'd made ours, some of the chaps would dry the used leaves and sell it to them as genuine, unused tea. Of course the Arabs became wise to this, in time, as the texture of the tea leaves, once they had been used, was far more brittle. We always had some tricksters, but I did not believe the ill will it produced was worth it.

Up to this time, I hadn't had any leave at all. Some of the chaps had had leave in Cairo before the battle of Egypt started. Four of us had not, and we were allowed to go and spend leave in Tunis. We were invited to stay with a French couple named Rabin who owned a wine merchant's shop. They made us very welcome, although we couldn't take to their idea of a fried egg running around in a sea of olive oil. Their daughter, a young schoolgirl, made quite a fuss of me. She had a smattering of English and wanted to learn more, though why she seemed to pick on me as teacher I don't know. They were wonderfully hospitable people, and we had a happy four days there, away from military life.

Come September, we were due to take part in the invasion of Italy, which had been kindly arranged for us. A landing ship arrived and was readied for us to put the tanks on. We knew we were going somewhere in Italy because troops had already landed in Sicily. We were told we'd better get some practice at embarking and disembarking from a landing craft. So we went on board and sat on long benches. Then we were told to disembark off the end of the ship, which we did, up to our kneecaps in water. We marched to the beach, and that was it, our training for the invasion of Italy.

1942 and 1943 Sea Routes to Egypt, Italy, and Back Home

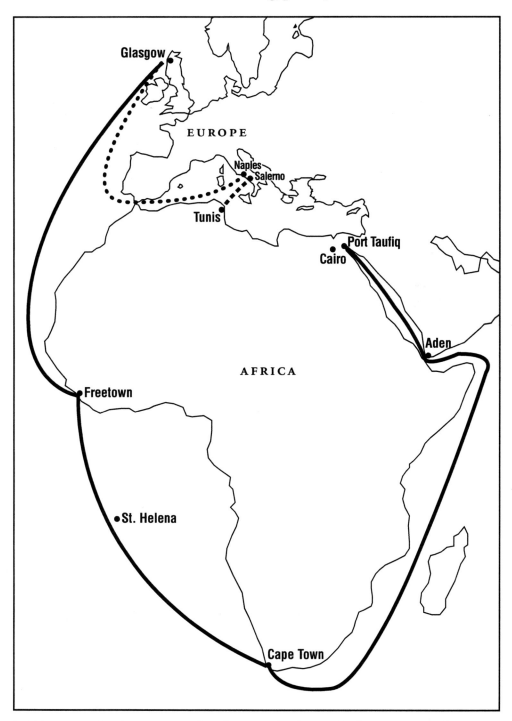

In February 1942, the sea route taken from Scotland around Africa to Port Taufiq, Egypt, was the only comparatively safe route for troops en route to Egypt. After the defeat of the Axis forces in Africa, the invasion of Italy at Solerno in September 1943 and a shorter route home in December 1943—Naples, Italy to Scotland—were possible through the Mediterranean Sea.

The Desert Rats

The 7th Armoured Division was first deployed to the Western Desert of northern Africa at the outbreak of war with Italy in 1940. While in Lybia, the division engaged in tactics of 'scurry and bite' against the enemy, which earned them the title of Desert Rats.

As their insignia, they adopted the jerboa (the desert rat) designed first as a red rat in a white circle on a red square (above), then later as a brown rat outlined in white against a black background (below).

The division served under Field-Marshal Lord Wavell, in which was originally the Army of the Nile. In 1941 in the first offensive against Marshal Graziani, they pushed his Italian forces back beyond Benghazi. Led by General Sir Claude Auchinleck the division fought in the battle

**Private Stanley Swift,
Basic Training, 1940**

at Sidi Barrani, the Battle of the Omars and Gazala. Later, as part of the Eighth Army, under the command of General Montgomery, it took part in the Battle of Alamein, the advance across Libya, and finally to Tunisia, which brought a victorious end to the African campaign.

The Division landed in Italy in September, 1943 and advanced northwards before being withdrawn early in 1944 to take part in the invasion of Europe. After landing in Normandy, it saw action in the region of Caen and Falais and fought through France, Belgium and Holland. Crossing the Rhine River it was part of the final assault on Germany.

Because of its illustrious record the division proudly marched in the victory parade in Berlin in July 1945. For the Desert Rats it was the end of a long, hard-fought campaign that secured them a lasting place in the annals of military history.

Desert Rats gun crew preparing to fire during the North African campaign.

British twenty-five pound gun in action in the Western Desert.

AN AXIS IS A FORM OF MILITARY SIGNPOST. IT DOES
NOT GIVE ANY DEFINITE DISTANCES TO PLACE
NAMES, BUT MERELY INDICATES BY THE SIGN THE
WAY FOR A DIVISION ON THE MOVE, BOTH IN AND
OUT OF BATTLE.
IT IS OBVIOUS THAT WITH SO MANY DIVISIONS AND
SO FEW GOOD ROADS, THAT WHEN A PARTICULAR
DIVISION IS GIVEN A CENTRE LINE (ROUTE) IT MUST
ADHERE STRICTLY TO IT, OTHERWISE IT MIGHT
POSSIBLY CROSS THE PATH OF OTHER DIVISIONS
ALSO ON THE MOVE, WITH CHAOTIC RESULTS.
THEY ARE LAID BY THE MILITARY POLICE WITH
FORWARD TROOPS SO THAT SUPPLIES COMING UP
BEHIND MAY KNOW THEY ARE ON THE CORRECT
ROUTE. WHEN THE POSITION GETS RATHER FLUID IT
IS VERY IMPORTANT THAT ONE STICKS STRICTLY TO
THE AXIS, OTHERWISE IT IS POSSIBLE THAT THE
WANDERER WILL FIND HIMSELF A PRISONER OF WAR.
AS THIS, OUR LAST AXIS STATES, THEY HAVE BEEN
LAID AND STILL REMAIN ALL THE WAY ACROSS
AFRICA, IN ITALY AND ACROSS THE CONTINENT.
THE EARLY SIGNS WERE MERELY A METAL
TRIANGLE PAINTED RED, BUT AFTERWARDS IT WAS
CHANGED TO A YELLOW TRIANGLE WITH A DESERT
RAT SUPERIMPOSED.
THIS PHOTO IS OF OUR LAST ONE PUT UP IN THE
SUBURBS OF BERLIN.

                    STAN.

(WRITTEN IN 1945)

From el Alamein to Berlin—the 7th Armoured Division 1942–1945

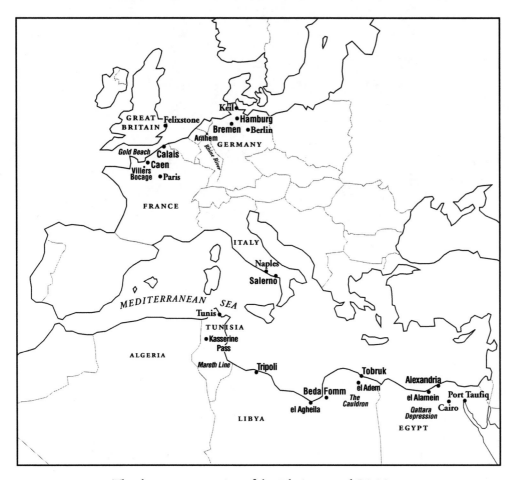

The three year campaign of the 7th Armoured Division.
Noted are the countries and places they took part in liberating and protecting.

Chapter 3

Italy

The journey aboard the craft took about two days, so we had a lovely Mediterranean cruise, all free. We landed on a flat beach at Salerno, which was surrounded by a semicircle of hills in which the Germans were safely ensconced. For the first three or four days of the invasion, they'd been giving the beach a terrible pounding. Fortunately, as we arrived the barrage had tended to quiet down a bit but was still pretty nasty. The thing was to get off the ship as quickly as one could and get off the beach equally quickly. Other troops, not as fortunate as our group, were having difficulty getting off their ship and were stuck on the beach instead of moving off right away. Thankfully, our lot seemed to move faster.

We were attached to an American outfit, and the German air force habitually came over the hills at first light, out of the sun, bombed the beach and, before you could get your wits about you, departed. It became an almost monotonous routine, but finally the impasse was broken. The Germans had had enough because another wing of the army, the troops that had landed in Sicily, was approaching from another direction.

The whole division had one particular road to start its advance. We were lined up, nose to tail, and the length of the division on that single road was twenty miles; the amount of equipment needed was phenomenal. We waited for several hours before we had the order to move. What a wonderful target we would have been for any roving German aircraft.

One of the great nerve racking situations was being on the road in a column and having to stay in line through a built-up area which was being shelled by the enemy. Ahead shells would be landing indiscriminately, and we had to run the gauntlet of that fire. As we got nearer and nearer, our nerves became more and more taut. We were going through one such barrage, and there was a huge crash to the side of us before we made it through. It was surprising that so many of us did make it, but it always tested our endurance.

We had great problems with land mines; there were so many of them scattered around. Once we were moving along a road when we suddenly came across what seemed to have been an accident. Gravel had been thrown all over the road. Now in a case like that, unless you were green, you went completely off the road and around it because the verges were mined and, underneath the gravel, mines would be laid, too. We had to acquire almost a sixth sense and trust to that and luck.

We had a most miserable three months in Italy. The weather was bad with heavy rains, and it was bitterly cold. We were struggling, over our ankles in mud, trying to maneuver guns. It's difficult to manhandle a gun in those conditions, to struggle and sweat and strain with the damn gun acting most difficult. The terrain of Italy was not conducive to aiding an attacking army. As soon as we circumvented one mountain range, lo and behold, there was another one behind it. As soon as we cleared Germans from one range, ahead was another one. Half a dozen Germans in a position like that, on a mountain, could hold up a whole division for days. We were wet through, clothes and bedding soaked, and we had no opportunity or facilities for drying them.

We had one comfort. Our stalwart chicken, Daisy, was still with us. Having endured the rigors of thousands of miles across Africa, grubbing around in sand, she now encountered most fertile earth. One day, lured by the verdant growth, I suppose, Daisy wandered through a hedge to the next field where other troops were camped. When we realized she was missing, we searched for her. Alas, the neighboring troops had already got her plucked and in the pot. Our Daisy! I only hoped in her Elysian life she remembered us with affection.

The Germans must have thought that the method they'd devised in the desert of skidding bombs along was highly successful. At one point we were temporarily housed in a square block building about three stories high. From the main track, which wasn't much of a road, ran a long, raised path leading to this building, in front of which sat a stone horse trough. Early one morning another chap and myself were outside the building when an enemy aircraft tried this trick of skimming along almost at ground level and releasing the bomb. The plane seemed to come out of nowhere as our view was obstructed by trees in the area, but when we heard it, we both dived behind the horse trough. The bomb dropped, skidded along, and bounced straight over the building like a tennis ball, landed in a field on the far side, and lay there like a dying animal. Fortunately, it had a time fuse, and from every doorway of the building, soldiers poured out as if they were off to a football game. All were well out of the way before the bomb exploded.

The next day I was walking along the path leading to the building, carrying a box of rations on my shoulder, and once again an enemy plane flew in low, firing cannon. I shot down between the bank and a gun we had in position there. Suddenly, there was such a whiz and a bang. I looked up, and there was a half-inch cannon shell embedded in the breech of the gun. Guardian Angel number four!

A few of us were pulled out for a rest and were allowed to go on leave to Capri. American forces had occupied it as a rest and recreation island. We stayed at a hotel there, a couple of chaps and myself, and rode up on the funicular to the piazzas and cafes on top of the island. At one cafe there, we spent all the money we had on cherry brandy at threepence a tot. We were well away by the time our money ran out. We hadn't a penny left to ride down on the funicular afterwards, so we walked, which was a sobering experience in more ways than one.

At the hotel, one of our chaps became ill one evening after over-imbibing. The next morning at breakfast, a waiter brought the man's false teeth into the dining room on a silver salver, they having been rescued from the toilet. A touch of class indeed!

Then it was back to reality, back to the rain and mud. As part of our kit, we were issued with gas capes, long, shapeless garments designed to shield us in case of gas. We found these very useful as macintoshes when it rained. When we slept, usually in the open, we put these capes over us, covering our faces, too, against raindrops. One particular night, I found a suitable bed space in the track of farm vehicles, an indentation several inches deep and wide enough to fit myself into, and crept in under my cape. During the night it poured, and in the morning I found myself floating down the track, so much water had filled the rut. Everything was sodden, and the problem was we had no hope of getting anything dry, week after week. That must have been one of the worst winters Italy had had for a long time.

A couple of days later, we entered a village and found a smithy there. It was quite warm inside, the embers from the fire still hot and glowing, a god-sent haven after the cold and rain outside. So we decided to sleep there, congratulating ourselves on finding such an inviting place to bed down. Unfortunately, we were not the only ones to bed down there. In the middle of the night I awoke, bitten to death by fleas, big as coconuts they must have been and numbering thousands. My face, trunk, arms, and legs were a mass of bites. They had had a feast. I must have looked a gruesome sight. I had to flee that snuggery and spend the rest of the night on the ground outside. Some other chaps joined me. The rest must have been very heavy sleepers.

In our advance, our column was stopped in a village, just a minor stop for a short while. We had a driver at that time named Jenkins. He could have passed as Ronald Coleman's double; he had a thin moustache and was very fond of himself. Actually, he had something to be fond about as he was quite handsome. While we were stationary, he saw a girl leaning out of an upstairs window of a house. What unspoken invitation he'd received I don't know, but he left the vehicle and disappeared into this house. Shortly afterward we got the order to move. Jenkins was nowhere to be seen, and so the sergeant pushed me into the driver's seat of the vehicle and said, "Drive the damn thing." Now my driving experience in the Western Desert had been brief and hardly skillful, so I maneuvered as best I could. About three or four miles further along, when we were again halted, driver Jenkins came sprinting up. He'd begged a lift further back in the column, and here he was, tardy but, I suspect, unrepentant about the cause of his delay. I gladly gave up the driver's seat. He was in dire trouble for that call of the wild, but he seemed to feel the crime was worth the punishment.

We moved slowly, painfully northward. We were stationary in a gun position, waiting, having been called to a halt, and Rispin and I started prowling around, seeing what we could sniff out. We walked away from the guns and came upon a dead German, face down on the ground. We made mistake number one: we turned him over. Very often bodies were mined, and if you disturbed them, that was the end of you. We had been foolish but fortunate. I took a wallet from the man's pocket. It contained letters, in German of course, unintelligible to me, and photographs of a family, a young woman I assumed to be his wife, and children. She would get the inevitable telegram. Suddenly, it all became so personal. It wasn't just a German corpse, it was a human being, a family man with responsibilities and concerns, just the same as us. I slipped the wallet back in his pocket.

The second mistake we made was that we put ourselves in view of the German observation. A few shells came over, not many, three or four, to warn us, and we took their advice and hurriedly departed. We had made two fundamental mistakes and got away with both. Odds were in our favor that day.

At one time we were in an open field which was a bad site with no cover. I was trying to get some sleep one night when a shell came over and landed right at the end of my bed. It didn't explode. Guardian Angel number five. Sometimes you wonder.

While in this same field, an enemy reconnaissance plane came over and that meant trouble. Someone had a wonderful brainwave and said, "We'd better move." So we moved about two fields further away, and lo and behold, several hours later our former site was heavily shelled. A cat and mouse game.

About the beginning of December, we were near to Monte Cassino, the monastery high on a hill that was later utterly destroyed by the American air force. (They bombed it, and bombed it again.) American and Polish forces were trying to gain the high ground, and Polish troops had been ordered to capture the position. In reality, half a dozen Germans could hold that ground against a whole division, and the Poles were being slaughtered. Imagine trying to take a fortress of that kind, on top of a precipice. It was well-nigh physically impossible. The great courage shown by troops in that assault was almost unbelievable. Today the memory of that battle and those who gave their lives lies in the extensive cemeteries on surrounding hillsides.

We were then pulled out of action because it was rumored we were going home. We could hardly believe it. We were dog tired, worn out, at the very limit, and little did we realize what we were going home for. We withdrew southward and, just before Christmas 1943, were given a short rest at the resort of Malfi, previously a holiday spot for Italians. We had the best time we could have had under the circumstances. We even got up a small battery dance band with a pianist who was the major's driver, a trumpet player, and a drummer. Surprising as it may seem, for that short period of time, I was the vocalist. As I stood there singing, I was transported to some top-notch place, the band all in black and me resplendent in a white jacket. Ah, imagination! That week or so of rest was a recuperative time away from war and the constant tension of knowing you are in range of the enemy's guns and aircraft, far enough away to experience peace without the ever-present fear. It was a wonderful, healing feeling.

But good things come to an end. We marched to Naples, looking for the ships that were going to take us home. All our equipment was lined up, and a Canadian division came to relieve us and take over our stuff. They didn't know what to do with it. We'd fired thousands and thousands of shells from those guns. Everything was completely worn out, ready for the scrap heap. We left the dilemma up to them.

Our ships duly arrived, and surprisingly, it took only two to three hours for us all to embark and the ship to set sail. On board we were assigned to an area where we ate and slept. A large table stood fixed to the floor, and at night we slung hammocks above it. It was a most comfortable way of sleeping as we moved counter to the ship's motion and felt no sway, as I'm sure every sailor knows.

On Christmas Day we stopped at Oran, but we were most anxious to get home as all sorts of fiendish thoughts were entering our heads. Of major concern was would the Germans be waiting for us when we went through the Straits of Gibraltar? Luckily, we encountered no enemy, and now we set our sights on home and England.

Chapter 4

Europe, D Day to Berlin

Ye arrived in Scotland in almost precisely the same place from which we'd left, so long ago, it seemed. Now we were real, battle-hardened warriors, but in truth, the whole division was absolutely exhausted, battle weary. It seemed hard to expect us to embark on the invasion of France as a spearhead, whereas most troops who were waiting in England had not had any war experience at all. They were being trained for this specific endeavor and were what you might term *green*, not in any derogatory sense, but they were inexperienced in actual warfare. We were experienced, and our experience was essential.

We went sent by train to a place called Brandon in Suffolk, which was in the middle of nowhere. We were billeted in Nissen huts, miserably cold as it was the beginning of January. Fortunately, a few days later we were given leave, and for a short time, I was reunited with my wife whom I'd not seen for two years. I was able to tell her how her letters and the knowledge that someone was thinking of me had been the thin strand, the lifeline I'd clung to because there was always a feeling of loneliness out there, even among so many men.

Then it was back to Brandon and the start of training once again. We now received new guns. They were still twenty-five pounders but were mounted on top of a Sherman tank chassis, which made them self-propelled. The Germans already had quite a lot of these, and they were highly mobile and very efficient. So we came upon this idea second. We even got the idea from them for jerricans, which were utilized for carrying both petrol and water and were a wonderful piece of equipment, very versatile.

These self-propelled guns were protected by a three-quarter-inch shield of steel, not a lot of protection as the shield was only about three feet high but more of a psychological comfort.

Training was different now because it was in closed country; the southern part of England was accessible only by the military. We had a certain amount of recreation time and on our off-duty hours went into the town of King's Lynn. The country by then was packed with troops and equipment ready for the invasion, particularly these southern counties.

There were about a million American troops stationed in England at that time, and every Saturday night saw battles in the town's market square as everybody poured out of the pubs. Americans and British would rough it up, but I kept out of it. I'd seen too much of battles. The problem was these chaps were so fit, so well trained, they had to get rid of all that energy, so they took it out on each other—the amount of liquor they'd imbibed fueling certain built-in resentments, real and imagined. The military police would wade in, swinging batons, no matter who got hit, to break up the fights, but the next Saturday night it would start all over again.

Time drew nearer to the great invasion date. We were moved to Ipswich, near Felixstowe, which was to be our point of embarkation. There we were encamped, and as the great day drew nearer, the camp was suddenly encircled with barbed wire. There we were, prisoners. Up until then we'd been allowed to go into the town of Ipswich in the evening but now no more. So what did we do? We happened to find a heavy garden roller which we threw into the barbed wire, then crawled through the gap and escaped. I think the powers that be were afraid we would reveal information to roving spies, but we were no threat. We had no specific knowledge of military plans.

Work continued, and all the vehicles were sealed so that we could land in water with the tanks. This was a messy job but finally done. We put the vehicles and tanks on the hards—vast paved areas where vehicles were parked awaiting transport to war—at Felixstowe and prepared to embark on the landing ship.

What a highly organized operation that was! Men in bowler hats with clipboards ordered each vehicle along. One vehicle in the long queue broke down, and almost unbelievably, it was immediately pulled out and an identical replacement pushed in right away. It was a phenomenal exercise in meticulous planning.

Multiplied by all the ports in southern and eastern England in which the same operation was taking place, it was nothing short of miraculous.

Our location was the furthest away from the French beaches, so we had to start early. We had a false alarm as we were ordered to set off on a particular day, then everything was postponed for twenty-four hours. So we waited, once again on an American ship, an LST (landing ship tank), controlled by an American crew. We pushed our tanks into the hollow cavern below, and we, to the best of our ability, sat up top. While waiting on board, we had American food, and it was excellent. Those fellows certainly knew what good rations were.

We finally received word to go. Many LSTs were on the water. We crawled along, partly up the Thames estuary and down and round until we got to the Dover Straits. The Germans, either through radar or visually, saw our convoy, and they had some great siege guns with which they used to shell Dover. Of course, they weren't feeling very friendly, and a lot of these big shells came over. The nerve racking problem was that we could see the flash of the gun. Then we'd start counting. At a certain number, the shell arrived, and there was a terrific clatter. Although the Dover Straits looked rather narrow, we realized there was really a large expanse of sea. Unfortunately, one of the ships was hit, and it happened to be carrying fuel. It exploded in an almighty fire, a beacon for miles.

It's hard to describe the feelings I had on that comparatively long journey from Felixstowe to the beaches of Arromanches [Normandy], France, not knowing exactly where we were to land. The gamut of emotions one goes through, of fear, anxiety, thought of the unknown, were the same feelings I had had approaching the war in the Western Desert. Would I survive? Would I let our side down? It's the uncertainty, the not knowing.

We carried on and got to our target on the afternoon of D Day. The invasion had started, and as an armored division, we couldn't land until the beach had been cleared. The engineers had to clear the beach of all obstructions, mines, steel bars, and all kinds of hazards. As the beach was mined, they had a horrendous job, with many casualties. The paratroopers had already landed. The sight was incredible; it was almost impossible to see the sea for the number of ships. Men-of-war were slinging great shells onto the coast, the RAF was bombing, rocket ships were firing hundreds of rockets from their batteries. It was an awe-inspiring sight, frightening and yet wonderful. The sea was rough, and our LST was bouncing around like a cork. There we waited all night, and the following morning we got the order to go ashore [at Gold Beach].

We were ordered onto the beach. I saw bodies in the sea moving slowly backwards and forwards with the movement of the water, like long-stemmed seaweed as it undulates in the swell. The tanks were in a tremendous hurry to go forward, no one showed any concern, and they simply ran over whatever happened to be in the way.

Amazingly, I walked off the ship and hardly got my feet wet. Things were fairly quiet. Infantry had made inroads for about two miles, but it was a very precarious time, touch and go. Our first day was pretty uneventful. We made our way through the town of Bayeux, and then we waited for instructions and the rest of the equipment to catch up with us. We couldn't go further until the whole unit was ready to move off as a fighting entity. We were then ordered to hold our position in order to let reinforcements get in behind us. It took several weeks before we could even be sure we would be able to stay in that part of France; the situation was still very fluid.

This is how we were organized. We were a troop of four guns, closely allied. The battery itself was eight guns, and there were three batteries in the regiment, for a total of twenty-four guns in the regiment.

An individual troop was close-knit, just four guns often working in isolation from the rest of the regiment. We had a gun position officer who received instructions from the officer detailed to spot the targets and work with the tanks or whoever demanded his services in front, well in front, sometimes. This was a position nobody relished at all. He was the observer.

On the gun position itself was the gun position officer who, if we had to make a move to another location in the country, went in an advance party to find the best site, preferably one that was somewhat hidden from the enemy. It wasn't wise to place guns in an open field for everybody to see, if one could help it. So the officer chose country with a certain amount of cover, trees, et cetera. Of course, we couldn't fire under trees because the shell might hit a tree and burst, with dire results for us.

After he found a suitable place, we were ordered to advance to it and were given a map reference. There we'd position the gun and drop the ammunition limber to the side of the gun while the driver departed to the wagon lines, as we called them, further back. We were all in radio contact. The gun position officer set up a tent or cover of some sort and laid out his artillery board, and with that and other instruments, he would assess our target, determine range, et cetera, and issue instructions.

Sometimes when the terrain was difficult, we'd fire a smoke shell as the officer on the gun position had to take into account the barometric pressure because this affected the drift of the shell. Each artillery shell had a copper band around its base, and the rifling in the gun barrel bit into the soft metal of the band. This put a spin on the shell as it came out the barrel, which always caused it to drift to the left; nobody knew why. This had to be adjusted. Then we commenced what we termed *ladder fire*. If the shell had burst too far and was difficult to track, we dropped the range until we could see it, then we bracketed the target until we were relatively accurate. If it was a moving target, we had to quickly adjust the range, downward if it was moving in our direction.

A quick thumbnail sketch of our gun crew—our motley crew of five. Sergeant Eason, a stocky granite of a man from the Gorbels in Glasgow, was the toughest of all. He bragged about the number of venereal diseases he'd had as if they were Nobel prizes he'd been awarded. He had a tough exterior but was really kindness itself.

Then we had bombardier Garrett, a handsome man whose skin had the pinkish bloom of youth. Quiet and rather taciturn, his claim to fame was seducing a woman he'd once met briefly. This seemed a casual encounter carried to extremes.

Then there was yours truly. I don't know what my comrades thought about Gunner Swift, skinny lout. He was an excellent gun layer, though. Once in the desert, before we were decimated, we had so many rounds to fire. That meant we had ten shells to fire quickly, and after each shell was fired, I had to do my job and re-lay the gun on its correct line with instruments. We finished firing before our sergeant's archrival, Sergeant Short, and his team did on their gun. Our sergeant acted like a little boy who'd won a prize at school. We'd beaten them! They were still firing, and we'd finished. We'd beaten them! He was treating this like a huge childish joke. I suddenly cracked and really lit into him. His jaw dropped in amazement because I'd never been one to pass any comment or bite or kick up a fuss about anything. I think it dawned on him that this wasn't to be looked upon as a childish prank or a game to beat each other. This was serious business.

Gunner Bawley was a young lad of eighteen who came to join us as a rein-forcement for the losses we'd suffered. He was what we termed a swede-basher, a true country yokel, kindly, juvenile, not understanding anything going on around him. He bit or sucked his top lip persistently. I was ordered to teach him the art of gun laying, how to use the instruments, but it seemed beyond his comprehension. He was a nice lad who should really have been in school.

There was Gunner Severn who dealt with the ammunition. He came from one of the coal-mining areas near Nottingham. He was a peculiar fellow whose legs seemed to go one way and his body another. Nothing seemed to coordinate. He was efficient, though, and did what he had to do.

I must not forget poor Gunner Clarke, the man we lost. He hailed from the east end of London. On the very day he was killed, he showed me photographs of his wife and child. I learned more of him in those few minutes than I'd learned in all the time we'd been together. It was as if he had a premonition. And when he was killed, I thought only of his wife and child.

Then there was our driver, Broome, who was a rotund youth with flabby, red cheeks. He came from Milwall, east London. He talked forever about the Milwall football club. He was a joker, which kept our spirits up, and he was a useful adjunct to the team as he drove us—drove us mad, sometimes.

As a crew, we were not overendowed with courage. I was always prepared to dig a hole whenever we stopped for any length of time, even though we might have to move on in the next half hour. There was always another hole to dig somewhere further on.

Some of the reinforcements that came to us when we returned to England were not aware of this sense to take all possible precautions. One wanted to come home without any great damage, at least physically, and one had to take care. Dead soldiers are no good to anyone and not very comforting to relatives. Some did take risks and were soon to suffer the ultimate fate.

One laddie had joined our unit in England. During this time when we were held up, he didn't bother to dig a hole and, instead, slept in the vehicle. Unfortunately, the vehicle was under a tree, and during the night the Germans dropped a great number of anti-personnel bombs, which were released from canisters and spread all over the place. One of these hit the tree and exploded, and that was the end of him. When I awoke in my little pit, there were marks of personnel bombs that had exploded very close. We had learned from experience that if you were below ground you were relatively safe, apart from a direct hit, so it made sense to take what precautions you could.

—————

Orders came for us to move forward and try to probe into what might lie ahead. Our destination was a place called Villers Bocage. We went along quiet country lanes. There was nothing there; the area was peaceful and serene. We camped the night just outside Villers Bocage. It was ominously quiet.

The next morning a small group, not the entire division, went through the village, which was just a main street with houses and shops on both sides. A German Tiger tank had backed into one of the shops and could not be seen as one approached down the road. Once again the Germans displayed a macabre sense of humor. The officer in charge of the tank waited there, sporting a top hat on his head and above it an open umbrella. Our tanks went by unaware of this spectacle. The officer let them go through, and when the soft supply vehicles carrying ammunition, et cetera, came along, all hell broke loose. This Tiger tank fired on them and destroyed virtually all of them, setting them afire. Our tanks were then trapped and couldn't get back. All the men were taken prisoner. It was a wonderful piece of military strategy—well organized, when everything had seemed so quiet.

We had apparently bumped into the German Second Panzer Division, which had returned from the Russian front, been refitted, and given a period of rest before we hit against them.

One great problem we had was that German anti-tank guns were waiting and could hear our tanks approaching. Now, for men inside a tank, their vision is very obscured, but it isn't wise to stand up in the turret and show oneself. In this heavily covered ground, dense with hedgerows, we lost a hundred tanks one morning in a matter of hours. Tanks so easily caught fire. Tommy cookers was what the Germans called the Sherman tanks because they burned so readily after being struck by an anti-tank shell.

We placed our guns in a field and defended our position, constantly firing at the enemy, who were all around us. We had to wear triangles of bright fluorescent yellow nylon over our shoulders so the RAF and American planes could see where we were and not bomb us as we were in such close proximity to the Germans.

I was sent to reconnoiter, and in a corner of the field was a stunted, mis-shapen tree. I climbed into it and was able to look over the hedge in front of us. There were German infantrymen coming through the neighboring cornfield, quite casually. I reported back hurriedly, and we received the order to fire the guns. We got them down to zero, attempting to fire shells into the adjacent field. The Germans had cut the road behind us, no supplies could reach us, and we ran out of ammunition.

There we were, now defenseless, surrounded by the enemy. A huge siege gun on Mont Pinçon a few miles to the south of us was dropping so-called *dustbins* every few minutes with a terrific crash. In the midst of our dilemma, the brigadier appeared and said we had instructions to retreat. Thank God for that! We were to move out that night. As covering fire, the RAF would come over and bomb Villers Bocage.

Dusk crept upon us. The RAF duly arrived and pulverized the village. It was immoral, really, but necessary. The din was so intense it drowned the sound of our tanks and vehicles moving out. Friendly tanks had come up from the rear and sealed off the side roads in some way so the Germans couldn't cut the road as we pulled out.

One man in each vehicle was to guard the rear of the vehicle with a rifle, which would protect the vehicle behind. We had a little pip-squeak officer who had come as a reinforcement and had not had much experience. In fact, there were two such officers, and we nicknamed them Tweedledum and Tweedledee. They were full of their own importance. This officer ordered me to break the rules, ignore the instructions we'd been given, and guard the front of his vehicle instead, I suppose as a way to protect himself. This I refused to do. There was no protection for the vehicle behind us in such a position. He was most angry and said he'd deal with the matter later.

When we finally retreated, deathly tired, exhausted, I pulled my sleeping roll off the vehicle and laid it out. I can't even remember lying down. I was out. Some hours later when I woke up, a chap asked me if I'd heard the raid. Apparently, a German fighter had been over, machine gunning the area. I'd been oblivious.

The next day the pip-squeak officer reported our incident to his senior officer. Not surprisingly, that earned him a stiff reprimand, not me. I believe that taught him a lesson.

A stalemate set in. It seemed almost as if things were developing into what had happened in World War I. We couldn't move forward; we were blocked. It's difficult to describe military jargon, but apparently, the Germans were pivoting on the town of Caen. This was one locale militarily that they were not prepared to give up. We were just stuck there—it seemed forever—at least for several weeks. General Montgomery kept making excuses for our lack of movement because pressure from politicians and press was growing. General Patton and the U.S. Army were going around the edge and galloping forward with little opposition. This put us in rather a bad light.

We camped in a field a few miles from Caen, and the RAF bombed the town time and time again. According to later reports, there were really no Germans in the town itself; it was the civilians who suffered. Many were huddled in the cathedral which, fortunately, wasn't completely destroyed, but there must have been an awful loss of civilian life.

We in our position kept firing. Other units joined us, and in the end, the area became absolutely crowded. The place looked like a fairground, bursting with men and equipment. The supposedly non-existent German air force—according to the media—came over and bombed us. There is a distinction between the bombing of a city, where you can feel a slight degree of hope, and the bombing of an area, where the enemy is aiming specifically at you.

For psychological reasons it was always more nerve racking to be bombed in the night. There is a great need for self-preservation, coupled with the wish that you could see what is happening. I never felt the same degree of anxiety when we were being bombed in the daytime because you could see the direction of the plane and knew from the trajectory of the dropping bombs whether they were going to be near or far. But at night, you counted each explosion as the cluster of bombs fell, each one getting nearer, and you hoped the last bomb wouldn't hit home. By that time we'd had a long war. We were getting no sleep and were tired beyond the limit of endurance, yet nothing seemed to be happening. It was the soul-destroying endlessness of it all.

At this time I felt that my nerves were getting on top of me. I wasn't able to sleep, even in the small pockets of time we had. We had to fire harassing fire on the Germans to keep them awake all night. Of course, the powers that be forgot that it kept us awake as well. Concerned about my condition, I went to the doctor, who probably had seen more than he ever cared to see. He gave me tablets. I think they were placebos; they did nothing for me.

One night I was crossing the field as German aircraft started dropping anti-personnel bombs in the vicinity. They probably weren't all that close, but at night, sound carries and is much clearer. I saw the blue flashes and heard the huge crack of them exploding. Suddenly, my nerves failed. I collapsed on the ground, crying, helpless, unable to stop. I was shell-shocked, completely shell-shocked. I lay there, curled up, crying like a child. The medical man came but didn't really know what to do. He gave me an injection which put me out, something to make me sleep, I think. Afterwards, I felt somewhat ashamed, but my condition apparently had been understood.

The next day I was taken off the guns temporarily and put on the quarter-master's tank, which was a relatively safe position to be in, just liaising between the tank regiments and the guns. It was a position less fraught with danger, but I didn't really relish being there, and I seemed to have recovered sufficiently to want to get back to my unit. In retrospect, I realize that a man who fights on when his nerves are beginning to shatter is as courageous as a man who, by nature, feels little fear. In fact, any man who says he isn't frightened under fire is either a liar or a maniac.

For a short period, I was put on a vehicle as a rather inexperienced co-driver. I struck up a friendship with the man who was the driver, a chap named Smith who came from Macclesfield in Cheshire. Again we had little Tweedledum in charge of the vehicle. I thought, "This is going to be ridiculous," and I said to Smith, "This officer is going to get us killed. I'm asking to be moved." So I went back on the guns.

And would you believe it? Later this officer lost his way, away from the rest of us. He must have gone somewhere on some mission or other, lost his bearings, and couldn't find us again. He apparently instructed Smith to go down a lane where anyone with any experience at all would have smelled a rat. When all is so quiet, the silence so dense you can cut it with a knife, that is most dangerous. The vehicle rounded a corner, and there in waiting was a concealed German anti-tank gun. The disadvantage is that the enemy can hear you approaching, but you can neither see nor hear him.

Immediately, a shell struck the vehicle, and Smith was badly wounded. The officer and the rest of the crew managed to climb out of the vehicle. The officer ran back down the road they'd come, and the crew of four was taken prisoner. The officer then ordered a tank, which he encountered, to go round the corner because there was a problem. The tank rounded the corner, and a shell hit it in midsection and set it on fire. What cool thinking. What strategy. Smith was carried away on a French farm cart and died some time later. My words had proven prophetic.

Yet a strange thing happened. The crew from the vehicle had fallen into the hands of a group of German SS (Nazi elite guard), and they talked with them, telling them that the forces against them were so huge it was impossible for them to win the war. They talked them out of further resistance and convinced them that their only recourse was to surrender. They then marched their German captors back under escort. Captors became prisoners and prisoners, captors. Two of the crew got a military medal for that. It was a tragic but also funny episode. Such is war.

Finally, the day came when we did break out by dint of hammering away at the enemy. We started the long trek, and once we got out of a particular war zone, the country was unbelievably peaceful and untouched. It was incredible to experience, as though war had never existed. Everything within the area of the coast and up to Caen had been destroyed, smashed up. What a feeling of relief and pleasure it was that we could perhaps rest for a short time and figuratively recharge our batteries.

So quickly did we advance as the Germans fell back to the river Seine that lines of communication became stretched, supplies were not able to keep up with us, and we finally had to stop. We were out of petrol and ammunition. We were rationed to about three shells a day. God knows what would have happened if we'd been attacked.

We had four guns in the unit, and two were pointed one way and two the other as the position was so fluid. Two or three miles away we observed some Germans towing guns that were horse-drawn! We fired one of our shells at them over fairly flat country. I felt sorry for the horses.

So we waited.

Halted as we were, knowing there was no possibility of immediate move-ment, another chap and I had the idea to go to the nearest village. There we found a cafe, but I can't say the locals were particularly welcoming. They were quite a sour-looking lot, but then it's no wonder. Anyway, we partook of the local wine, perhaps too liberally. We started back to our encampment, but we couldn't find the field where our guns were. We supposedly had a ten o'clock curfew, and there we were, still searching at eleven thirty, as far as we could determine in our pleas-antly befuddled state.

The next morning we were hauled up before the field officer, a serious-minded chap, full of pomposity and military law. We were sentenced to 180 days confined to barracks. Confined to barracks? In a field? What a laugh! It was all right with us because we weren't going anywhere anyway.

There was a tacit understanding that everyone, officers and men, dig their own trench. One day German planes came over, flying very low and machine gun-ning. I jumped into my trench only to find Tweedledum already in residence. I took unkindly to this and said a few choice words. Consequently, I was up before the field officer once again, only this time it was junior who had a strip torn off. He was told to "dig your own bloody trench. Holes are for one tenant only."

We always had an air force liaison man with us who called up airplanes when we were held up at any particular point. Typhoon planes would be rushed in, and they did appear amazingly quickly. On one occasion we were held up by an enemy tank which was dug in on the edge of a wood, and within less than an hour, Typhoons came over and rockets went straight to the given target. In that space of time, the tank had moved, so the rockets were wasted, yet it did prove the accuracy of these aircraft.

But accidents did happen. One time a Canadian division was in front of us when large numbers of American Flying Fortresses appeared. German anti-aircraft guns started firing but at an angle. Shells were bursting while the Fortresses were over the Canadian troops. All the bombs came down on the Canadians, annihilating many.

It was getting on in the year, and a large RAF airport just outside Brussels, Belgium, was bombed to hell. All the planes on the ground were destroyed. We had fought our way into Holland and were resting for a couple of days, but we were always prepared to move, and we never knew where we were going to sleep at night. If we could get under cover, it was a miracle.

A chap and I came upon a shop, an empty shop as there was nothing to eat. The woman who owned the premises was living there, and she was kindness itself. She made us some small doughnuts, even though she probably had nothing to eat herself. Such acts by these war-torn civilians were touching, and we were most grateful.

It was my birthday, September 1944, a dull morning, and one felt the first chill of approaching winter. I saw hundreds of planes towing gliders, and these three airborne divisions were to be dropped to facilitate the capture of three bridges: Eindhoven, Nijmegen, and a further one at Arnhem. This was Montgomery's plan to enable the army to thrust through into Germany and end the war by the winter.

American forces quickly controlled the two rear bridges, but the bridge at Arnhem was too far from support. It is essential in all these operations that ground troops arrive quickly to consolidate the position. Unfortunately, the airborne troops ran slap bang into a German armored division. Also, unfortunately, most of the roads in Holland were raised above ground, and the land around fell away, giving no room to maneuver if the road became blocked.

We were sent to consolidate their position, originally, but it quickly became apparent that the best we could hope to do was rescue them. It was too ambitious a project. We, as a convoy, were in full view of the enemy and were heavily shelled. They kept hitting the road behind us so that we were stuck there, going neither backward nor forward. The remaining men of the airborne division struggled back across the river, and later we, too, had to withdraw.

Then it was the middle of December. Although, according to the local grapevine, the enemy had nothing left in the way of arms, suddenly the German army appeared from out of nowhere in the Ardennes in Belgium and started to attack [Battle of the Bulge]. As it was a week or so before Christmas, it seemed most unfair of the Germans to mount an assault then.

Christmas was bitterly cold. We six in the gun crew found a billet in a small farmhouse with an elderly farmer and his wife. They had just one cow. They must have been so very poor, yet they were kind beyond measure. We sat in their front parlor, and they made us a roaring fire with a kind of briquette, coal dust cemented together or some such material, and the room was roasting. They brought in pastry, jam tarts, and the like. They couldn't do enough for us. We tried to reciprocate by giving them tins of bully beef, which was no problem for us.

We had been given an issue of rum in winter, but instead of drinking it, we had hoarded it, and on Christmas Day in the farmhouse in front of the blazing fire, we dispatched the lot. There was two feet of snow on the ground, and I had to go outside to answer the call of nature. Sometime later, the revelers noticed I was missing. Lucky for me, they came out and found me sitting in the snow like a zombie. Apparently, the cold had hit me, and there I was, full of rum, oblivious to my plight. I could have frozen to death! So they dragged me in and put me to bed. Merry Christmas!

Just after Christmas we got the order to move. It was still bitterly cold, so cold that when I put my fingers accidentally on the tank, the skin stuck fast to the metal. We had an advance tank about a mile ahead of us which would radio back to us any targets it could see so that we could fire on them. This tank came to some open ground and, unbeknown to the crew, there was an anti-tank gun in the garden of a house nearby. In front of the open ground, the enemy had laid mines. Our observation tank ran onto a mine, and there was a colossal bang.

Now, such an explosion shudders you, and your brain ceases to think as it rattles in your skull. We were trained that, if a tank hit a mine, we were to bale out, get to the back of the tank, jump onto the tracks the tank had already made, and run back along the track.

The tank crew was miraculously unhurt, but one chap, dazed, shaken by the explosion, got out and made a basic mistake. He jumped off the side and landed straight on a mine, which blew him back onto the side of the tank. As a consequence, we were forced to back out. We came up against some resistance, fairly firm resistance. We exchanged fire and waited and exchanged fire again. After about three days, we broke loose and advanced over the same ground. There was the damaged tank, with the remains of the chap frozen on the side.

And this is how it was. This is how it really was. We tried to find a lighter side to all of this whenever we could. I think we were sometimes manic, but we had to find jokes, to find a laugh somewhere, sometimes, or we'd go stark, raving mad.

We became immune to human suffering, death, and dying. We came upon a German officer who had walked onto one of his own landmines, which had blown away most of the bottom section of his person, and he had shot himself in the head with his revolver. But even that hadn't killed him. So we put him on some sort of support, and he lay there, making animal noises. He was taken away, and I never saw him again. He was a human being in dire stress, *in extremis*. What can you think? What can you feel?

We were once ordered to bury some dead German soldiers who were in our area. The ground in Holland at that time was like concrete. It was impossible to bury them in the normal way, so we found a quick way of disposing of them. We pushed them down a well, out of the way—without any qualm, without any conscience.

Later, something of a thaw set in, and we were travelling over half-frozen mud. All the vehicles on the move were churning up this slippery muck. Our tank sank up to its hub, and our driver cursed but could do nothing. I didn't really know what I was supposed to be doing on the tank at that time. I was assigned to the machine gun, but I'd never fired it and didn't know how to. The Germans were shelling this very spot because it was where the rest of the division had crossed over, and there we were, stuck.

A tank stopped in front of us and let out its hawser. My officer ordered me to get out, grab the end of the hawser, and hook it on to our vehicle so that we could be pulled out. I didn't take very kindly to this as shells were falling. There I was, up to my knees in freezing mud, struggling to get the heavyweight cable attached. God, what a life! And who said there were no Guardian Angels? By a miracle, the shelling stopped. I suppose the Germans had had enough. So had I, as slowly we crawled ahead.

We came upon a small village, just two streets of houses and a church. We had to take control of the church spire because church spires were obvious points of observation for the enemy. When we saw a church, the first thing we had to do was demolish it and get out the Germans, who were inevitably there. When we took command of an area, we would try to protect these sorts of observation posts, naturally.

I was on guard duty, and when on guard I always felt it unwise to stand out in the open and show oneself, so I positioned myself as close to a wall as possible. A German soldier appeared at the end of the street, and bullets from his automatic weapon came whizzing past. Thank the Lord I was well concealed and not in the line of fire.

Later, a German patrol came into the area. We in our crew saw them coming from a distance and dived through a window into a sort of church annex which had remained intact. We watched and waited, and the patrol just walked by and back again. We weren't crazy enough to fire on them; that would have been the most foolish thing to do. We didn't care to face Germans close up in that sort of situation. No, not one bit. We preferred our enemy a few miles away.

When in action, if you happened to be sleeping, the slightest noise would wake you instantly—no half measures, no drowsiness. You'd be instantly alert, every nerve on edge. I awoke in such a way one morning when I heard a plane approaching. There was ten-tenths cloud cover, and I could instantly smell a problem as it was almost certainly a reconnaissance plane. By a million-to-one shot, as it came through the cloud cover to have a look, the anti-aircraft gun hit him. He came screaming down and landed in the field next to us. We went across and saw that the plane had buried itself three-quarters of the way up, with just the tail showing from a hole in the ground. Another soul gone. Another German less to fight.

In most of the villages, civilians had fled because of the proximity of war, but as the action passed and things quieted down somewhat, the villagers drifted back. We were resting in one such village, and on the far side of the road from our position, a family had just returned to their house, and I noticed a young girl, obviously a child of that family. She appeared to be about ten or twelve years of age. I see her to this day as she stepped beside the garden path. She trod on a land mine. The result was too horrendous for me to even chronicle. Her mother came running out of the house, and she lost her mind. She became crazy, demented. I doubted that she would ever recover.

We finally crossed the Rhine on a Bailey bridge the engineers had built, leaving behind a country much flooded as the Germans had opened sluice gates, allowing sea water to enter.

We entered Germany. It was an almost anti-climactic experience as I recall no exhilaration at being on German soil at last. The Germans had been so battered that their situation was hopeless. We went into a German village. Our tanks had set fire to the few houses there, just to be on the safe side in case there were snipers inside. The German women stood outside in the street, watching their houses go up in flames. There was no pleasure in witnessing that, no pleasure at all.

Some German prisoners were delivered to us. They were all elderly men, and they were frightened out of their lives. The propaganda had been at work, and they thought they were going to be killed. They shakily offered us their rings, their watches, whatever they had. We were absolutely astounded. One man asked me to take his watch, and I said no, I didn't want to have it. I offered him a cigarette, and the look in his eyes of disbelief and thanks I'll never forget. The propaganda, the enmity, the hostility of past years drained away all in a few minutes. I think we both realized an unspoken truth: we were no longer enemies.

In villages, many of the German houses, we discovered, had cellars in which food was stored. Fruit and vegetables, often preserved in jars, hams, eggs, sometimes quite a bit of food laid away there. We were resting in a village, and I came upon a large ham. I was ever the improviser. Nearby was a dump with all sorts of junk tossed into it, the sort of dump you'd find almost anywhere. Into this dump someone had thrown a big iron copper. I thought this would be an ideal receptacle to boil the ham in. So I poured water into this rusty copper, found material for a fire as there was plenty of timber and rubble about, and set my spoil to cook. Half a dozen German women stood nearby, looking agog at the proceedings. I pointed to my wristwatch and then to the ham starting to simmer, pantomiming how long should I cook the thing? The women appeared to think this was a huge joke. It was surprising how the barriers came down. Anyway, with or without their help, we had a wonderful time consuming that ham. It lasted us for days.

We fought our way on to Bremen, attacking it with artillery fire, and at last the town surrendered to our forces. There we learned that military plenipotentiaries were negotiating for the surrender of Hamburg. Certain German officials, it appeared, showed fighting spirit and wanted to let all the civilians out. We were not prepared to allow that, of course. The civilians would be our bargaining tool. The Germans were then informed that there were four thousand of our planes standing idle, which was no understatement, and they could pound Hamburg into rubble if they didn't surrender. After a lot of cogitating and negotiations, it was agreed to surrender this important port, and on May 3, 1945, the capitulation of Hamburg was official.

As far as we were concerned, the war in Europe was at an end, but the genuine surrender terms were not signed until General Eisenhower dealt with them.

We left Bremen to someone else to sort out, and with the overwhelming feeling that we have survived, that we have come all this way, thousands of miles, and we have survived, we continued on our way and crossed the bridge into Hamburg. In one of the buildings on the side of the road on which we were traveling was a German sniper. Nobody had told him that the war was over. He shot and killed one of our officers who was sitting on top of the tank. I reckon I witnessed the last man to die in Europe. It's strange how some people's luck runs out. He could have killed any one of us.

We ended our journey at Lunebürg Heath and then moved north to the Kiel Canal. Everybody in the immediate area was turned out. Nobody was concerned about finding accommodation for those people; they had to go. It was May, so perhaps it wasn't too cruel an edict. I got to know the youngsters in those parts. There's no vice in young kids; they're the same the world over. We arranged with their mothers to do our washing and ironing. They even cut the tails off our shirts and made them into new shirt collars. They were good to us, and we paid them a pittance.

In July we were ordered into Berlin to take part in the upcoming victory parade. We were housed in the old Olympic Games stadium on a hill about two miles from the center of the city. German women came in each day to clean, make our beds, et cetera, and I was put in charge of these women, assigning them their various jobs. I was also made battery clerk. Because I made up the lists for guard duty, I didn't stand any guards, which caused a certain amount of resentment, naturally.

On 21 July 1945, Prime Minister Winston Churchill and Field Marshal Montgomery along with other military men stood on the saluting base in Berlin. The Seventh Armored Division was given the honor of playing the principal part in the victory parade that marked the end of World War II.

After the event, I saw a young mother on the street pushing a pram with a baby just a few months old. I paused to admire the child. The woman told me its name was Paul—that much I could understand—and also that her husband was either still in the army or had been killed—it wasn't clear to me which. She was there alone. There weren't many men in Berlin at that time, only old men or men minus limbs. I gave her a bar of chocolate for the infant, although it was obviously far too young for it, but it was treasure to her, it seemed, for she broke down and cried. Once again it came home to me so poignantly that, all the evil and propaganda aside, when people meet together, despite problems, despite the language barrier, they can become friends. I wanted nothing but to see someone happy.

After the victory parade, a club was set up for us, called the Churchill Club. We could buy tea, cakes, and sandwiches there, and there was also a quiet reading room. Once a drunken Russian soldier came in and started firing into the ceiling. Everybody dived under tables as we were all still battle edgy.

Occasionally, we wanted to stay out late at night and would employ the old trick of laying a stuffed kit bag in our bed under the blanket. The duty sergeant nipped around quickly, giving only a cursory glance over the room. One night, pretty late, I was walking back to the barracks and was accosted by yet another drunk Russian who pointed his gun at me, demanding cigarettes. In fear of my life, I gave him a packet, and he started hugging me and wanted to give me a wad of paper money before he staggered off into the night.

Outside the ruined Reichstag, a market was set up, and everybody bartered goods. If we had coffee or cigarettes, we could get anything. Anything. People offered jewelry, wristwatches, whatever they had. There was always a vast crowd present, and cigarettes and coffee were currency. We had some villains in our gang, though. Cigarettes came in round tins of fifty. These chaps would open a tin, cut the cigarettes in half, fill the bottom with waste, and place the half cigarettes on top. Unsuspecting folks thought they had a full tin.

But many of the Germans were starving. Our waste bins into which we used to sling all the food we hadn't eaten were a mecca for these defeated people. They picked out and took away what they could, and as winter drew on, those people did suffer.

One day in Berlin I noticed a girl, and because I had been without feminine company for so long, I just stopped and spoke to her in the street. She knew some English and, as we became more acquainted, filled a need in me for friendship. I was married, and there was nothing else in it for me other than that. I think it is understandable that, after all those years of male company, of such a closed community of men, I craved the company of a woman. Perhaps I misled her; perhaps she thought she was in love with me. I even met her parents. I got great pleasure from giving her little gifts, food we had leftover, cakes, and chocolate. She said to me once, "I don't understand you. You give me these things, and you don't want anything in return." And I didn't. Those things I could so easily get prevented her and her parents from starving.

The time came when we were posted away from the regiment we'd been with all the way from the Western Desert in Africa to Berlin. We were posted to a holding regiment from which we were going to be sent home for discharge from the army. We were issued with a number relating to our age and length of service. My number was twenty-five.

While in this holding regiment, we had to guard prisoners. They were civilians who had been rounded up and put in a huge camp fenced off with barbed wire. This camp was a former shoe factory, and as the weather was bitterly cold, these people would march about, trying to keep warm. Women were in one compound, men in another. As far as we knew, none of them had done anything particularly wrong, but they'd been rounded up to be vetted.

We patrolled along a catwalk between fences, and visitors would come there, mostly to weep. I was stationed on a raised platform, just like in films in which the guard stands with the gun, only I had a searchlight which I used to flash intermittently at night to see if anybody was moving about in the yards.

With time, we got slightly acquainted with some of our prisoners. Women in one compound had husbands in the other, and officially, they were not supposed to communicate with one another. They would occasionally try to sneak a letter through, and depending on how we felt, we would surreptitiously get this letter to the other compound. It seemed a humane thing to do, and they were very thankful. These people were finally weeded out, and I believe most were set free. It was post-war hysteria. Anyway, most of the officials running the country at this time were ex-Nazis. The country needed to get back on its feet, and they had to be re-employed in their former jobs.

The day came when it was time for me to leave. It was Christmas day 1945. Many other chaps and I piled into a broken-down German train with no windows in the coaches and traveled all the way from Germany to Calais, France. Some chaps were on luggage racks, some were on seats, and I and several others were on the floor. The journey took days. We went through Belgium and Holland and crossed the bridge at Arnhem that had been so badly bombed we could feel it creaking under the weight of the train.

Finally, we arrived at Calais in the midst of a severe storm. We settled into a holding camp there to wait it out. The weather was so bad that floating sea mines were being tossed onto the beach and exploding. It seemed ominous; the war had not gotten us, but might we get done in on the last trip of our army life?

The weather eventually calmed, and we were shipped across to Dover and told we were going to York. The night was freezing. We arrived in York at two o'clock in the morning, and the barracks there were icy cold. There was no heat, no nothing, just bunk beds with an empty palliasse, which we had to fill from a great pile of straw before we could get some sleep.

The following day we had breakfast and later went through the demobilization process. Everything was laid out: suits, jackets, trousers, shirts, tie, trilby hat, socks, underpants, undervest, even collar studs and cuff links. The lot. We were measured, visually, and I chose a gray pin-striped suit, produced, like thousands of others, courtesy of Monty Burton's, the tailors. Everything was then packed into a box. It was all yours.

We signed ourselves off. We were free men. Someone said to me, "Good-bye, Mr. Swift." *Mr.* Swift? I looked around. Who did they mean? Then it struck me. Gunner Swift was no more.

We went through the gate to the street. Spivs lined the way offering to buy our boxes. I doubt there were many takers. Still in uniform, clutching my new civilian wardrobe, I caught a train to Nottingham and arrived in the early hours of the morning. And so I came home, six years less two months since the day I'd left.

I had to rouse the family. My wife had been discharged from the WAAF earlier, and she came hurrying downstairs. Later her mother woke up and made us a cup of tea.

There were no flags, no bands, no neighbors cheering. I had come home, and now I was expected to go to work and pick up the threads of my life from where I'd left off. It was hardly possible. I had two weeks free, but it took me at least two years to become adjusted to civilian life. That was true for many of us, I believe.

The problem was we had to start thinking for ourselves. For years everything had been thought out for us; all we had to do was obey. We had been fed, clothed, and paid, and I came home with thirty-five pounds in my pocket. Now we were on our own. There were no special programs or assistance in recognition of our service, no educational opportunities to improve our prospects. We had served our country, and that was that.

I emerged from all of this without any great physical scar. I stood up to what was thrown at me fairly well, I think. I didn't wilt under pressure. But it was long, so very long, all the way across Africa, into Italy, through Europe from D Day to Berlin. One has only so much courage, so much resistance. There were days when I was depressed, days when I felt I wouldn't see it through, days when things were hard and difficult and I wondered how long before I, too, succumbed. But I am a firm believer in that Guardian Angel. Why did I survive? Why was I allowed to come home?

I recall when we were badly bombed in France and nerves were frayed and almost ready to snap. We could hear the tank men praying aloud. I admit that I, too, prayed silently that if I could be spared, O Lord, I'd be a good man. If He'd allow me one night of peace with my wife, I'd forever be a good man.

I was allowed that night of peace. A good man? I try.

I remember.

It was indeed a lovely war.

Epilogue

And what about it all? What about all that we had fought and died for? Yes, we had conquered a monstrous evil but at great cost. I've often thought since of the sheer madness of mortal combat. I've thought of the thousands of shells I was responsible for firing from that gun, and I hoped to God I had injured no one. It was an impossible hope, I know, but I never saw the results of my actions; they were always five or six miles or so away. I can't believe that I didn't kill or maim someone. But was I more responsible for that act than the person who drew up plans for the gun, or people in foundries who molded and made the gun, or workers in factories who filled shells with explosives? Was I more responsible?

It was a terrible trap we were all in, but we had won. Contrary to popular perception, although we had masses of equipment, much of it was inferior to the enemy's. When the war began, Hitler was prepared, all his equipment up-to-date, and ours was antiquated. Until we could catch up, it was inevitable that we could not start winning, until 1942 when things gradually improved.

We were in many cases outgunned, both in the efficiency of the shell fired and also in the range, which was most important. Our adversaries were hitting us before they were in range of our guns. Our twenty-five-pounder gun was an excellent gun of its kind; vast numbers were produced. But it had a comparatively short barrel and, therefore, the muzzle velocity was very low. In fact, you could stand behind a twenty-five-pounder gun, see the shell leave the gun, and follow it as far as you could see. By contrast, the Germans had an eighty-eight gun which was very versatile and had a terrific muzzle velocity. It was used initially as an anti-aircraft gun, and then the Germans recognized its value as an anti-tank gun and also as an artillery or field gun. The velocity from this gun was so great that it beat the speed of sound. The shell arrived out of nowhere, and we'd hear the gun fire afterwards.

Our anti-tank guns were very small, owing to our late start, but we did develop six-pound anti-tank guns and, I believe, seventeen-pound anti-tank guns, in the end. Also our tanks were not up to the German equivalent. German tanks, especially the Tiger tanks, were very heavily built and almost impossible to penetrate. Early British Valentine tanks had two-pounder guns and were totally inadequate. The Honey tank was a little pram of a tank, and the American Grant tank had a gun on the side which was immovable so that, in order to aim the gun in the right direction, the tank had to be moved around. The Sherman tank's build was very high, which made it an easy target, and it caught fire so easily. Imagine a crew trapped in a burning tank. If you've ever heard pigs squealing in their death throes, that's the noise you hear.

Such inadequacies took a toll on the crews. One cannot imagine the terrible strain a wireless operator in a tank goes through, sitting inside this awful tomb, not knowing what's going on outside. The static noise over his headphones and the, perhaps, panicky instructions he's receiving cause an unbearable strain on the nervous system. I think this led to many problems later. The psychological aspect of war had never really been closely monitored, not enough for people to realize not only the physical damage that is sustained but also the mental damage from the horror of it. Men were driven crazy by the shelling and bombing, shell-shocked to such an extent that they were useless. What sort of a life they would have afterwards, provided they survived, is impossible to tell.

We learned, but the lessons were painful. With the arrival of the Americans, we did acquire masses of equipment but much of it no match for our adversary's. Our divisional general, who was a good man and had been with us all the way from the Western Desert to Operation Overlord, complained about the inadequacy of our equipment. He was sent home and bowler-hatted.

And we ran out of human beings. We were out of tank people almost one hundred per cent. In fact, near the end of the war we ran out of infantrymen. Orders went out to scrape the bottom of the barrel, and we were raking in all sorts of odds and sods for the job: engineers, anybody who could hold a rifle. Fortunately for us, we had to stay on the guns.

Casualty figures are always somewhat shrouded in mystery. Thousands died at el Alamein alone. The story goes that, on his deathbed, Field Marshal Montgomery said to a friend that he was frightened of facing the Lord. His egomania was fading away as he lay there, and he added, "What will all those men I ordered to be killed at el Alamein say to me when I cross over?" His friend, to reassure him, said, "They'll welcome you. You did a job that had to be done." Yes, he did.

I often think of my comrades who fell by the wayside. We had a regiment that totalled 600 men. Out of these, about 250 were killed. I don't know the count of wounded. Yet that was good; we were lightly let off. Tanks and infantry lost many, many more. Storming the beaches on D Day, in the first two hours a company of infantrymen was reduced from 213 men to 23. Now these are real casualties.

I have visited military cemeteries. Reading names inscribed there told me what I already knew about the sheer obscenity of war. I think of my friends whose bones are resting in the desert, such an alien, terrible place to be, and of their relatives who read those dreaded words and wondered how they died. Death is not like a cinema story. Death is horrendous. The body has no protection against terrible weapons, and shrapnel tearing into you is no respecter of persons. Men who have been badly wounded, who are dying, come to the realization this is to be the end of their young lives. The look of fear, the return to an almost childlike state, this is what I remember.

Yet in that valley of death, there is only one thought, that of the preservation of life, one's own. You have to close your mind entirely to only one thing: the sooner you kill your enemy, the better chance you have of surviving. You have to strip yourself of any thoughts that he is a living person and has his problems, just like everybody else. You have no idea who he is, and the sooner he is out of the way, the sooner you can go home. That is the basic truth. That is what it's about. That is what we felt in the Western Desert. The only solution to our ever getting out of that godforsaken place was to eradicate the foe. I never hated Gunner Schmidt, but a faceless enemy had to be eliminated. It's a contradiction hard to accept.

My experience of war was something I wouldn't have missed yet wish I could have missed. The ultimate contradiction. It changed me considerably, and nothing else seemed quite as important as it had been before.

We can't live in the past. I don't believe in nostalgia. Nostalgia is a belief that everything in the past was beautiful and pleasant. It wasn't. But I believe in remembering. This war I shall never forget.

Index